THE END

Published by Sidebrow Books
P.O. Box 86921
Portland, OR 97286
sidebrow@sidebrow.net
www.sidebrow.net

©2019 by MC Hyland
All rights reserved

Cover art by Cinta Vidal
Cover & book design by Jason Snyder

ISBN: 1-940090-10-5
ISBN-13: 978-1-940090-10-8

FIRST EDITION | FIRST PRINTING
9 8 7 6 5 4 3 2 1
SIDEBROW BOOKS 021
PRINTED IN THE UNITED STATES

Sidebrow Books titles are distributed by
Small Press Distribution

Titles are available directly from Sidebrow at
www.sidebrow.net/books

Sidebrow is a member of the Intersection Incubator, a program of Intersection for the Arts (www.theintersection.org) providing fiscal sponsorship, incubation, and consulting for artists. Contributions to Sidebrow are tax-deductible to the extent allowed by law.

THE END
MC HYLAND

SIDEBROW BOOKS • 2019 • PORTLAND & SAN FRANCISCO

Now I feel ok about saying "my life" while knowing for certain it's a kind of bauble reflecting other baubles and so on in a series.

—Lisa Robertson, "The Cabins"

THE END

I got my period in the specialist's office. Little whoops of a siren somewhere nearby. Light comes in from the corner. *Sui generis* something or other. You don't need to understand the process. Bored but canonical. Under all the floor tiles a camera keeps its secret. I beamed through time and into this kitchen. An arm touched and unfamiliar. A cloud of many small changes. When you get to the end you reverse and push off. Keep adjusting the dosage. Wait in line to enter the dimly lit room. We come up against a boundary in our affections. Would you call it a spiritual instrument. What did your vocabulary really do to you. Sometimes my body is too discursive. All scraped with morning light among the riches of the gas station. How in those years taste became a precondition. We went where *uptown* indicated elevation. To think more about your senses and less about your feelings. Certain indoor panics. Friendship unclarified by the conditions of city life. A line down the block. I didn't want to be part of your movement. All the tiny cuts half healing. Metallic streamers in the Mexican bar. *Life of the mind* in a way I suppose. Another day another line. We stayed to watch the lights change slowly. Complacency of the brunch hour. Problems of bodily leakage. Long white fluorescent lights slide by overhead. Sometimes you think of a person all the time for no reason. Flashing off a cell phone screen. Respiring or repining or expiring. Where the social ends and the political begins. A little festival.

THE END

Someone must have said *we want prisons not colleges*. Evening comes on fast. Petrochemical film on the skin. A wink of sky glimmers through a boarded-up garage roof. An inventory of effects. All the humiliations of having a body. I want to know what work is. Listening to your mixtape. I said *the typewriter*. Sirens heading south. Somehow the *OED* becomes *The Economist*. Server error. Morning light. Is this a form or only a strategy. You were no special snowflake but your particular pain flooded through me. Is it load-bearing or cosmetic. All the windows cracked. Would you consider this an amplification. The plane's trajectory hard to chart from sound alone. The mystery of the irregular polyhedron. No bright line between one state and another. Just a certain weariness as if you've worn out your eyes. Tools of a revolution. Who do you know. I could tell it was morning by the artificial harp. I bought her the t-shirt. Looked at all the photographs. Hissings and clanks. Scrapings and clanks. How the season changed without our notice. How to think about friendship and liberal individualism. This is what we call conceptual practice. A right ratio of ankle to shoe. I wanted to know where you go when you think. Sound of the digital camera shutter closing. The internet is down again. A life of post-economic facsimiles of labor. Filtered light through the blue curtains. A dispersed atmosphere of small compromises. Today's snowflakes shrink and disappear. Landscapes reverting to forest.

THE END

Some things I think of as outside and inside that might be only ambient. Open an aperture onto the morning. Tinny feeling all under your skin. Autoeroticism as autodidactics. Infant-size noise-cancelling headphones. I lost all my footage when the phone crashed. The prism disrupting its own light beam. Filmed the sky out the train window again. Tell me about your secret job. The shushes of cars make clear it's still raining. In one of several possible futures I hear you exhale from the shower. Try not to think of all the things you touch. Bells in the background. Sprung up before the light. A vocabulary of no-longer-quite-right words. The scarf smells like her for years after her death. Are you bleeding on your new leggings. New people in the lobby waiting for their movers. The second old-fashioned made me puke on the tiles. One light box to another. The prescribed situation of video projection. You practice conversation to make it perfect. Walked to the post office. About the effects of late capitalism. Sometimes facts get melodramatic. I'll probably never see him again. Kiss on the cheek I notice her teeth. Then a voice says *crazy ass Brooklyn ass shit*. We cunningly decorated our need to make money. Knowing in advance how the collaboration will sour. Everyone's getting sober or divorced. No one wants another disposable tote bag.

THE END

My friend gave me this mirror so I could think about her while I look at myself. Slow tears reflect in a windowpane. Can you think the thoughts of elsewhere once you've lived in this city. Perhaps a question of mental discipline. I slowed down and smiled. The next thing I knew I was buying commemorative keychains. The difference between a lake and an ocean. You shiver all over the beach. Were the seagulls as big as you remember. First I saw the tall green spire. Dreamed of our wedding in a ski lodge or dorm. Sometimes only the smell will tell you. I don't like to put on lipstick unless I'm on a subway. How a blue sky appears gray through sunglasses. Breaking into the Hen Do market. *Plan for campfire* means *pack Febreeze*™. Authentic Southern Home Cooking. Boarded up. Ambivalence of commemorative street renamings. She wrote *I am such a good girl. Such a fool.* A New Year without the internet. How alive the dead seem. I turn a page and sneeze. Take the other stairs. *A sketch can have the function of a skirmish.* Rain in the airshaft. A stranger made me question my favorite font. Three generations on a bus sharing chicken. The sad thing about history is everybody dies. A war's memorabilia right outside the garden gate. Then we crest a hill past Newark. Small bits of fluff float around outside the windows. *Vague heartless chase/ Of trivial pleasures.* Bachelorette's Night Out. When you read *I held his shoulder and touched a fat soft bump* you know where the story will end. Water stain spreading across the living room ceiling. Plastic bag crinkles. Maybe at the next block we'll be able to see the sunset. The walk changes every mile so you know where you are.

THE END

Help yourself to a tiny cheese snack. Bombs over Gaza. Bombs over Donetsk. This is a kind of timekeeping. The year-old balloon still fully inflated. *We Are Working All the Time*. Lying right under the window fan. That one house with the severe topiary. Same newspaper on the bathroom floor. Then the women be like. Then the men. Forgetting what day it is by 2 o'clock. Look it up in the *OED* again. On the hand dryer someone wrote *I killed and ate my parents*. The difference between a coffee shop and a bar. Therapy so boring. Yoga so boring. Read the comment string about mascara with great focus and attention. Help yourself to the bread. Googled the obituary for cause of death. Student loan debt. Credit card debt. Garden of the Revolution. Mail system of the 19th century. Alleycat race on the coldest day of the year. Eating pretzels pulled from the trash. Wordsworth says the road is a better kind of school. Sound of sparks crackling inside the wall. New cracks forming in the ceiling. Make this night an event on a page. A high-end grocery store named Foragers. To call language a commons is to forget the kinds of rights people once had. Clear edge of the glass bird's tail. The fluid body of your vernacular. As though a place can be a tunnel through time. A picture of Robespierre's watering can. The trees grew up until all the vistas were blocked. In the blue matrix of how news stories spread. Take off your nightgown today for a change.

THE END

It's hard not to be a little bored with yourself. I would rather go blind by the closed-down Shake Shack. Being an adult. Having an accountant. Shuttering sound from a slide carousel. I never know when I mean *you* and when I mean *me*. Trying to find a new route north. You touch the metal bar near the ceiling. Memory function shuttled outside the body. You come in late holding an Ikea box. I keep the bar's neon sign in my phone. What about a band called 19th Century Pornographers. This mailbox is full. What is a monument. A question of how much feeling you can allow. Catch your breath once you board the train. Was it a media nostalgia or a media panic. Loneliness of having a body. How long the train takes coming home after midnight. Fear of French novels. 90s TV boyfriends. Dated the restaurant by its blue wall and knickknacks. Your viral slang performed in perfect accent. In the park across from the neon sign hotel. My own thoughts are hidden from me. It's hard not to find architecture boring. Voluptuous afternoon with a view down to the harbor. How many library books I've permanently lost. I saved the lyrics on my phone. Wiped them in the upgrade. All the checks my skin writes. Is there someone I can give this receipt to.

THE END

Don't be the white woman sobbing at the vigil. Type quickly before the screen goes black. More light. More mist in the window. We went to Union Square and marched or didn't march. We closed or opened our eyes into a communally willed silence. You join the reading group. What is there to say that can't be said in an email fueled by whiskey and rage. Shoot first and never ask questions. Traffic sounds. Late summer. Then fall. Then winter. Six months like that. For some it was the summer of cops. For some that happened every summer. Two saxophones and two black-eyed ghosts. How to be kind but also saying no. Saying *no no no no no no no*. Does the aesthetic have a political unconscious. Eyebrow threading en route to the protest march. We stayed up late refreshing our feeds. Putting the *media* in *social media*. Standing in the window. Then we have dinner in the brand-new Dairy Queen. A shooting back pain from carrying too many books. We were in Paris when the cops turned their backs. We were in Brooklyn when Paris got shot up. Another obliterating wave of ambivalence. The trains run all night. You don't have to be on them. Backpack full of foreign currency at the lost & found. I changed the SIM card back but texts kept getting lost. I write about my days because they're the only ones I lived. Writing *I am watching*. Writing *I am listening*. Here come the warm jets.

THE END

You made a little quiet in the rain. A coffee-shop failure. Whose enlightenment. Spring comes and you walk downtown. The lost water bottle. The lost half hour. What kind of life do you live in two cities. That was the spring everyone opened up their marriages. I was on the train trying to love everyone. Dead orchid blossoms all over the floor. Ana's mouth pressed on glass. A building-colored sky. Tried to love both with equal fervor. Snow then rain. If by *jetty* you mean *faux pearls*. Night in a bus shelter. *The Divine Comedy* as illustrated by Blake. I want to hear your music. So islanded into the night. I said it's hard to be a person and laugh cried. Why don't we have another Man's Ruin. Poetry superhighway. Poetry underground railroad. You wanted a workbook for being a person. Feeling around the edges of a life. Floral tinctures arranged in a curve and a bare tree in front of the window. But the Depression was in the 30s. Firewood delivery service. We walk almost all the way to the river past the Irish bar and Salvation Army. I know why we never dated. Science museum voice-over. To chat from a distance. How much biting will the hand that feeds me withstand. Time and space. Space and sequence. Cancun Bar. City Tool Rental. The windows fog and you go too far south. Make a mouth shape. When the air comes on. The deepest puddle. Blue night. Flat rate.

THE END

Ask me about authoring your own destruction. A little vernacular dribbled on your chin. How people thought before digital publishing. Family apartment in the West Village. Dropping down into various sorrows. I missed the train to the protest. TO READ ASAP. Failures of desire. Coyotes in the Bronx. Hand covered in grease holding shiny brass bits. Blame your aimlessness on where you live. Stay home and work instead. Balinese influence in the floral-pattern blouse. Let me be your emotional labor plug-in. Daylight savings. Two famous towers out the window. Blood in the snow where I am not. Isn't that Romantic. The ones with children. All that optimism. 400 emails in the inbox. To have been both a skeptic and a eugenicist. University flag. Women wailing and minimalist sculpture. An itch unlike that of pleasure. Everything pressed up against the 18th century. Cataclysm of battery power. How you tried to be in love. 1999. Jaggedness of female friendship. Unrepresentability of the home. Your poor ankles. My poor arches. I came to New York to get less famous. Standing awkwardly in the anarchist basement. Siluetas in the snow. On the couch clicking like. Poems or insomnia. Therapy or art. You put hearts where the eyes would be. I was having a thought emergency.

THE END

Folk songs of sexual violation. Move the furniture around. The knife always hanging there. In this case it's just a metaphor. Not acting from your higher self. I was old enough to be your very young mother. Asleep in the library. Asleep on the train. You were most interested in the acknowledgments. Other people's fluids. The mood elevator goes all the way to grateful. But I didn't know you were that tall. Watching bubbles rise in the seltzer. A warm place for your dick. Placatory in the streets and a bitch in the sheets. Reading Descartes on the train. I turn off the computer at 11. Me and my street harassment haircut. Having feelings. Amirite. How moving there saved your life. I'm making a space for all my friends. Run on the treadmill when you need to elevate. Sticky spot on the subway seat. I was on the bus. I was ornamental. You've been standing all day. Said *I'm not gonna give you my number because I'm married*. Sorry feminists. Sorry self. Walking dictionary of accepted ideas. An indistinct urge to take out the colored pencils. I was lost. It would be ok to frame the photograph. Trees reflected in a laptop screen. Sounds of rage from the bedroom. Friendship never makes me think of death. Trying to be a better kind of self. Sweet little commodity producer. Dang y'all.

THE END

Labor turns into money turns into cocktails. Thank you for shutting up. Is *going camping* a euphemism for sex. Taco time. I don't know why he was such a dick to you. Go upstairs and be the mummy. Where women fell from windows into the public space. Was he reaching up my skirt or falling down the stairs. This is a serious question. Filling notebook after notebook. Getting out of your own way. I bought your art before you figured out how much to charge for it. Found the poem on my phone. Man on the subway straddling an antique chair. When you travel it's nothing but walking and eating. Fennel and more fennel. I could tell from facebook that insecurity made them mean. Wanting to get away unscathed. It's ok to go home. Living life less consecutively. What kinds of voices do you let in. Asking for a friend. A butterfly clip. Walked through the supermarket with my hood up. Seriously a kind of privilege. Taste bud hallucinations. Her machine in two shades of blue. A little embarrassed by the term you coined. Night face. Game time. What kind of wiggle room is in the contract. Artificial flowers catching on my jeans. Whistle while you work. All I want at night is to be in the studio. Therapeutic walking. All my doubts. I can tell by the tone of voice you're talking to someone you love. Mocking the train announcement. Baby where you going. We're going all the way.

THE END

I looked *good* for a married woman. Missed the water taxi. Got my period at Coney Island. Is this getting funny yet. Every day a new body. Humans versus police. I am pressing the lump in my breast and I am not innocent. Touched all over by rage and hurt. Many ways of spying. What broke in your American dream. The white board and the gray wall. I hadn't signed the contract. Crumpled paper or crumpled daffodil. Leaving the facebook group. Pulled over in Long Island. On the subway I'm a man. Locked together and working. A calendar of blooming trees goes white pink green. How we might be made out of hearsay. The joke about my ex. My secret radical past. Your business school affect. What did we believe about careers. About influence. A studied neutral pleasantness. You know lots of girls riding bikes with their hymens. Who or what is the audience. Sending love to Lee. Sending love to Hanna. We have been asked to know how we know things. Trying to be everywhere at once. Walk right into the ocean. Water touches the container ship touches my foot.

THE END

I already knew about knowing you from twitter. We marched down Broadway. The problems of having a mom who wears fishnets. Is something burning somewhere nearby. We go to the beach. People mistake my silence for cool. Of course I remember TJ. Some story I once read. Artifacts pulled from the riverbed. I wash the table then sit down to fold the books. *That isn't what a pregnant wife would drink* I texted Erin. Unless she was trying to be discreet. Tonight it's the 1970s. The El and a city of matchsticks. It was because the artists needed the church's outreach most. I guess if you never pay your own rent. Tenement dreaming. When you get home you see the soles of your shoes crumbled to nothing in three places. How the city eats the things you put on your body. When *artist* meant *lost child*. T-shirt longing. Looking out the window at a dirty white wall covered with wires. Let me be your grammar plug-in. They were so poor so sick so ignored. An inventory of effects. Sarah and her graveyard. Tomatoes out of season. Is *wife* a life goal and how do I know if I've achieved it. Maybe when you die. How my left hip sticks. We sat in the intersection with Houston and cops hovered around us. Morning gut rot rolling over in the bed. Who do you protect. Some people are movie screens some people are projectors. Summer in Chicago. Babies strapped to chests. I rearrange the books then write all night. Because my twenties were snatched from the jaws of maternity. Did I forget to thank you. How the shelves sag and list. Put the needle on a record. This one goes out to everyone I know. An archive of interferences. She says *he's as sick as ever*. Then the fog rolled in so thick the parachute jump disappeared. Ian's poem in midair. Maybe nothing is easy. A midwestern space for privacy and silence. Where we can go to see flowers. They like to sleep that way.

THE END

Some people have names for the huge and terrible darkness inside them. Hello devouring father. All the mommies on the sidewalk with their bouquets. Sun on the harbor mouth from the train window. Habits of a life of limited cash reserves. Exchanging time not money for vegetables and studio time. Express train to the center. Pink snow all over the driveway. I go home to the beloved interlocutor. Sundress season. A question of care or skill. You had trouble controlling your eyes. What they admit or what they emit. Light falling to the bottom of the column. Pressing folded dollar bills into her hand. How do you communicate anything in words. Adamantly in support of wasted labor. Pro-ornamentation. How your sadness might get on me or get into me. Something like a manifesto. An experiment with liquid eyeliner. Happy America with her technocratic experts. I love staying home on Saturday. As though there could be enough coffee in the world to see your old loves in daylight. Pollen so thick it clouds the windows. More time than money. When I say *you didn't know me then* I mean *I didn't know me then*. Devouring father-shaped hole in the day.

THE END

Call your mother. I eat bread on the couch and stare at the radiator. Sadness of recognizing home from a plane window. The problem of learning who your friends will be. Low-level but persistent toxicity. What if the perfect poem has an infinitely small audience. Houses for feral cats made of plastic bins. You hate being the designated adult. Going up in the wonder wheel. Today is probably not the day we'll die. Trying like a teenager not to be too weird or to be the right kind of weird. Activism as a kind of amplified speech. Just 160 sheets of paper for a run of 150. I refuse to answer the email. I ride the train to the studio and film out the window. This is the part where a moon will exit my mouth. Were you the person I learned ambition from. Storyboarding all-nighter. Where the boat and the blimp can finally be together. He kept saying *it's all going to be fine*.

THE END

I can love you face to face but not on the internet. Inductive reasoning about what it means to be human. Fevered in a dead-end street. Poems jam the inbox. Of course the world is full of ambient awfulness. Sad state physics. In an uprising you must imagine no past and no future. This effort is ongoing and imperfect. Puddles reflecting trees. Little weeds poke up out of mud. What about a t-shirt that says *I Remember the Information Superhighway*. Puddles reflecting construction signage. How devoted are you to your performance. Dropping into character on the train. Defenders call this *mob mentality*. I guess I'm more interested in freedom of assembly. The people I know versus the people I *know*. Oil all over the coastline. How *working on your reading skills* might mean *working on your feelings*. Long catastrophe of the enlightenment. A body's limit is where it touches something not itself. Knowing as a speculative project. Drunk on camera sound. Going over the river again and again. Containers falling off ships in high seas. As if a person could be a diffuse film of consciousness spread over everything. At the edge of Brooklyn where they keep warehouses and birdsong. You go down easy like a baby. Phone call from an airport bar. You started to give off the Scent of Mortality. This seat is reserved. How to tally the times you vanish into a lit screen. Let's not get all sci-fi about this. History continuous or swerving. I can't keep a secret. I can't plan ahead.

THE END

Where the rain-filled parking lot shaded into the rain-pounded river. A vast expanse of moving gray. The problem is the thickness of the callus. As you fell you thought *it's ok I have health insurance*. Am I refusing to engage in the hopes of remaining unmarked or unremarked. Places where language comes to you. Where it deserts. It's time to be your other self. I seriously dreamed about killing children the night I got my period. I wanted to make over the doors and windows. Of course this is how the sun goes down. Through the thunderstorm that trapped you under an awning. Let's not mistake the bartender for a long-lost uncle. Trying to imagine how one could think of embodiment as incidental or secondary. When the old man pulled teenage me into an alleyway with a surprisingly strong grip on my left arm. Passing right below the threshold of notice. Bless me and god will bless you. Walking down the street in my shortest dress. To invite everyone in. What does it mean to escape ideological battles unscathed. *I don't want to do sex to you I only want to talk*. Can this poem be a compass toward something I am only starting to know.

THE END

Let me call you when I'm off work. The shirtless man sleeping on the church steps. The scar running laterally up his belly. Wanting the little spaces of freedom inside an absolute structure that flows between time and space. Your foot dragging in the river beside the boat. A little snag in thinking. How I finally learned my bra size. It's about everything else. The oiliness of good coffee. What goodness might mean and whether it has relevance for this historical moment. Totally administrated. Rooms for thinking or for fucking in. I hold my desirability tentatively and with deep ambivalence. Fly me to the moon. Sound of something unseen being dragged outside. The way *the market* might want something. What you learn about your clothing once you wear it outside the home. Sweeping the rug into some state of newness. Like hands on your windpipe. Like cold hands inside you. The pride I took in my own peripherality. Ethical stance of non-involvement. How you stood at the edge with your eyes all over everything. How fast and small every movement was then. When *my reputation* might mean *my paycheck*. Kids with cameras. Wanting to be pressed down onto a couch or bed by a stranger's nonsexual hands. Wanting to be held suspended. Counting the recessed lines of bricks and the cement windowsills. Even I can't hear voices from elsewhere so well anymore. Even I fantasized walking as an approximation of freedom. Liberty always in process and never achieved. Archived all your bodily aches as though you might appeal to them later. As though these cast-iron buildings might have had some other fate than condos and flagship stores. Pale blue all the way upriver. Rest your head on the oil-smudged window. Wanting to be a string of small acts of care. Laughter from the street below. The eerie familiarity of the man in the coffeeshop. What kind of work did you think these poems would do for someone else. Language making a small despair in the middle of the day like a hole into which you might breathe. I said as a poet I am naturally shy. On the bedspread on the concrete floor I tried to make a space for something new.

THE END

The year when all I read about was what it would take for the Gulf Stream to shut down. You know how the day will end if the computer isn't off by eleven. Becoming an ambassador of efficiency techniques. Holding it in. Whatever it is. Your posture veering away on the subway. The job that left you always at a deficit and the anger that moved around inside you while you did it. The process of writing is mostly a process of ego inflation and deflation. Psychic breathing. The way the sky is invisible from my living room window. You checked off the boxes that proved you were or could be ok. Some electrical hum. Debris on the stairs. How to count the number of trains you'll need at the beginning of the week. How to make a small economy. The pit of my stomach when I bought the health insurance. Three thousand two hundred and four dollars. A disagreement about whether saving money or paying debts comes first. What it would mean to resist the economies that threaten via withheld promises. How *credit* means *character* and who gets to have either. Car horns from outside the school or the gas station. Waking up into the conditions of shortage after the storm. I grew up with money and then I guess walked away. Sometimes when I think of the future all I can see is ocean. Dead zone in the Pacific. The Atlantic's trail of bodies and those bodies in history that crossed Earth's oceans breathing the open air. The difficulty of talking about conditions not feelings. Woke up like this. Looking for the dust cloth to give my hands something to do. The line between *a performance* and *a service*. How ten years passed without leaving a mark. The only motion today will be across this room.

THE END

Googled *the difference between description and naming.* Performing speech acts alone and in pajamas. What kinds of plurals live in this weather. Slightly slimy feeling of the skin while moving through the city summer. I cleared a space for rhetoric. Sun pounding down all around you. In the dream she was alive and ran a restaurant in a Queens row house. I sat at the table with composure. Is aging an effect of the body or of time. Little green strips laid end-to-end. New holes in your shirt. Drinking ginseng through a tiny straw. Her face was wider and more freckled. The opposite of winter. So hemispheric. Quoted the activist meeting while wondering how to define activism. How to articulate a position from afar. I remembered how he'd said *I'll call right back* and then weeks passed. How the new place fits you like a hand-me-down coat. The fountain dried up and the ache after a day on your feet. Artmaking as a voluntary and uncompensated simulacrum of labor. Working my way into productive discomfort. This helped me know what not to expect. I imagined a t-shirt and then there it was. The pair of dirty socks left on the floor. Violent rocking of the ceiling fan. All the stars I imagine outside the city limits. Cooperative. Cheerful. How the noise of the air conditioner drowned out the movie dialogue. The sunburn peeling in centimeter-long strips. Wanting to walk through the coolness of the morning. Knowing how to make the string tight enough. Most of what I saw was a pair of buildings I went back and forth between. A perfect photo of pastel apartment trim. The problem is my feet not my shoes. New Haven Style Pizza delivered in the Texas night. Googled *what kind of language is a description.* In the dream she regarded me pleasantly but without recognition.

THE END

The past's rage as the break approaches. Because of my gender I was playing the role of *material life*. I guess I wanted a way into myself. New shoes and new eyes. Ladies and gentlemen please be patient. *IT'S NOT A CRISIS IT'S A SCAM*. Could hear the train coming through the sound of crickets. I wanted to love you like a light slowly illuminating from underneath. Because having a body means doubting. All the tapping feet. Suddenly in the diner an entire ocean. Little liver that could. Lying on the floor breathing deeply. What I mean is. Is everybody comfortable. Something made me speak as though I were sure. How long is it permissible to grieve a lost love and when did he return to himself. Hearing the pitch of movement slowly rise. How darkness presses down above the well-lit station. *I need to find my own card* she said plaintively. What it means to survive. Is anybody hearing this. There were people everywhere willing to speak to and of power. High-speed lights from the south. How a revolution once meant something cyclical. Your aphorisms read twice. Breathing into the knot of pain. So many choices with negligible difference between them. We described the world we lived in as a borderless and teeming market. The thinking part and the stuff part combine to make a person. You carry the notebook. You keep showing up. Expired referral. Wind in your ears. All the poets on the blog trying to say what love is. A hand held to keep you upright. Sand all over the sidewalk. They are singing in the stopped train's car. The moon waxes and wanes. You knew in writing before you knew in speech.

THE END

Record sleeves warped and covered in mold. Train train ferry to the small hotel. How to step away from your life and seamlessly re-enter. Stay up all night before the flight. What your body does and what you will. I think *walking into a cloud* is a name for love. You had been at the bottom of a fjord for days. Feeling diminished by what you share with strangers. What I meant by *domestic* was *native to the region*. I sighted the path across the meadow. I was in college when this novel was published & therefore recognize its world as one I wanted but could not imagine. A small wooden sign. Scenes of the movie set in years when I knew those subcultures. As though photography had the witchy powers anthropologists claimed. The sadness of discovering adult life was not significantly different from what preceded it. Had walking become a way of seeing or a form of speech. Writing from the coast of her loneliness within marriage. Who is and is not an intellectual. How to lock up your brilliance in heterosexual commitment. I mean really it's all body body body around here. Squinting at my reflection to check skirt length. I was on the couch before the sun came up reading their statistics. How we had traveled through time and returned weeks later. The man's elbow resting on my arm & gut. All the brilliant men and their women at a dinner party in Paris decades ago. What does research look like. The tearing sound when something pries loose. I wake up early and write this poem without coffee or tea.

THE END

Picnicked near the *Don't Insult The Witch* sign. Broke the stove again. You learn a thing in one place and write it down in another. Wanting to get out into the world. Tight shoe or pregnancy. Here you are humming around the apartment and refilling various glass jars. When *they* enter the poem. Blurry & on the horizon. Who left these jackets by the stairwell. In the morning made of traffic and voices you sleep through hours of sunlight. Maybe this is a kind of diffuse epistolary novel. Smudge of paint on the keyboard. *On deadline* as a permanent state. On the wrong side of Fortuna's wheel & brimming with dailiness. Dearest liberty having taken you. Everyone adjusting their scarves in the new season. I liked the openly boring ones best. How could you make a poem into a tiny room. Predictors included writing or thinking. The carbon monoxide monitor beeps. How the coffee seemed to move around inside you reshaping your body in tiny ways. Almost too gentle to count as an allusion. Lingered on. How can I tell you what the afternoon has done. Holding his daughter's hand and looking into his phone. Still thinking about the problem of audience. Enthusiasm of a new friendship three drinks into the end-of-summer party. The word *social* indicates a certain kind of bar. To be at a certain place in life. What labor might mean to a given person. What might justice look like at fifteen or twenty or thirty or forty. How many times can I pull off this trick.

THE END

I believed I had reasons aside from nostalgia. Kept it cunningly concealed. Changing the water in which the beans are soaking. Waking to the sound of the police chopper. How did you learn to believe you would survive your heartbreak. Bedroom painted womb-red. Champagne wishes & real estate dreams. What morning means in your home. First comes love then comes marriage. Great relief of a day indoors. I am careful not to bump the perpetually sore bone while lifting my feet onto the couch. An argument on television in the other room. Like the time we heard gunshots nearby and froze in the hallway with our hands to the walls. The last day I saw him alive. The singer didn't know yet about the years of darkness ahead. They told me about the sound the tornado made as it razed the neighboring block. Getting used to the tightness of underused limbs. The pain of a retrospectively blessed moment. Why did I find the *YOU MAKE ME* postcard so romantic. Cowering in the hall closet. I believed all spaceships sounded the same. Fight or flight. Giving a child an adult name as an optimistic gesture toward the future. The plant has outgrown its pot. The plan is miles behind us. Portrait of the Artist as Overtaxed Slob. The sentences come in small clusters punctuated by periods of waiting. How to multi-task. Excitement of driving to the museum. First meal of the fall cooked in a huge orange pot. Climbing out of the shower I say *I told you so* silently to myself.

THE END

If you've run out of things to say you may need better ideas. Having left the city in a wheeled conveyance. It was one of several periods in a life largely ruled by hand-me-down leopard print. Lacking the whirl and swoop of her language. Airless sunset on the interstate. Advancing into a backyard filled with small white lights. I'd prefer it if *timebanks* were called *laborbanks* or *skillbanks*. Cut off by the tour bus. You haven't walked down this street for two months & now half the shops are new. No more cookies for breakfast. To always be working & never be finished. Electrical hum & air conditioner hiss. Becca says it's because we're living on the internet in real time. I knew I shouldn't be so scandalized. ALWAYS ALREADY PART OF THE PROBLEM. Itching under the skin of my arms. His mother could as easily have been one of my aunts. The erotic privacy of adolescence. Because in Coleridge it's all storms and feelings. The pleasure of telling tales on a mutually-reviled acquaintance. Parental fragility. I am a professional & therefore I did not respond with *lmgtfy.com*. Was poetry ever successfully an art of seduction. I'm speaking historically. How did I give off the scent of *caring person* & was it too late to change. What do you believe available for your poetry. Kings and Queens. I know I cannot properly see my own biases. As though the page were a container to be filled with the political speech of the moment. But really I came for the couch and the enormous glass of wine. Just another night crying on the subway. I've identified a large plate-glass window as a precondition for this afternoon.

THE END

We practiced wiping sweat from our necks. Every song reminds you of a person you once knew. Then the heat kicked on with much hissing and clangor. I had crafted a parasitic practice that transformed my paid labor into post-market froth. Was it a field or was it a city. I wanted to lie down at the edge. The breeze just before the train's headlight appears. You were making yourself a foreign continent. Feeling around the blunt edges of history. But medieval women may not have been so submissive. Standing on the sidewalk surrounded by luggage. Do you worry about what happens to humor when language moves away from a body. Is this getting too repetitive I asked though I was not even halfway done. Made an argument about the congruence of Lancelots. The children. The children. The protective phone case bought a day too late. I'd promised someone today would end. But somehow we found ourselves in Queens. Falling behind in the assignments you've set for yourself. Preferring to repair rather than to replace. Your body is so seasonal. Jo said *one was quiet and proper and one was a screaming wench*. Fluffing the covers and turning on the fan. Trying a new stairwell but finding nothing nothing nothing. Here I will comment on the flexibility of the form. A model of the world or a model of the self. You were watching it all with your microscopic eye. Sometimes you slip back into 2007 for just a moment. Memory of a hotel bed & whatever the opposite of seduction might be. I was trying to get it all down into words. Movement had become a precondition for air circulation.

THE END

Pushed with both hands against the promised land. Who approached the cathedral. I read the essay on my phone. Wiping tears away with less & less subtlety. Waiting for the moment the heat shuts off at 6. The speculative nature of global geography. Was it *In the Pines* or *House of the Rising Sun*. Capsized moon over Morningside Park. Pages falling from the notebook to the floor. You walked by the apartment dominated by a large wall clock. I was in your mother's hospital room. Trying to be a thinner membrane. Was this a memory or a dream. In the rose garden overlooking Long Island Sound. All this before the world changed. The large brown ceramic cup full of crushed ice and mint. We all pretended we were a boy becoming a man. We fantasized living in the boutique hotel. When the new millennium started in earnest. Printing up the tax records to take to the clinic. After receiving three drunk texts I thought *maybe I didn't say* my husband *enough*. Health care a persistent low-grade fever in the system. The work has no end point. All the young literary men out at the bar. Were you walking away or standing still. The day already past apex. Car horns and the sound of a plane passing over. Your summer my winter. Your morning is my night. Is there a word for the way the ghouls move down the aisle. Not walking. Not dancing. Being a stubborn and glaring stone. Having hunkered down in your refusals.

THE END

I couldn't tell if the book was a fascist fantasy or a paranoid fantasy. Omnidirectional violence. You can't just Urban Dictionary it. All the Christmas bulbs swaying on their fishing lines. Always on the edge of illness. I wanted to tell you about the Justin Timberlake song's instrumental rendition. I had packed pajamas and toiletries and left my suitcase in my office during the rally. Lying in bed and reading off your phone screen for hours. It's not a crisis it's a plan. Years later I suddenly realize the boundary he'd tried to set. Dollar bills taped to the wall & curling away. What is the relationship between the past the future the present. How to still this incessant panic. Wanting to hold your hand although or because I didn't agree with you. Was it a poem or a lab notebook. We wanted to be like tinsel moving slightly in the breeze. But also to lift our voices into the rapidly darkening park. I don't believe that these judgments are valueless. The photograph of the bar façade made something small clench in your torso. How you learned where your home was. I had to ask my students if I was using the slang term correctly. Resting your wrists on the cool cement counter. It's not a plan it's a coincidence. I had lost faith in the strength of professionalism. Instead I began class by talking about Beyoncé. We were crossing state lines. My body so full of history by which I mean chemicals. Wanting to know if geography means space. If history means time. The large Ziploc container of powdered cocoa. What did we believe about borders. It's not an opportunity it's a scam. Who slipped into the demonstration quietly and retreated into a police officer's car. You know what they say about paranoia. All the bloody seams slowly unraveling.

THE END

We thought we could crystallize caring. Watching the umbrellas going by in the street. Sarah calls this *studio time* although all we're really doing is thinking and making notes. I was worried about what I could no longer notice. All the beer distributors on their laptops at the counter. I made a note to watch for epic similes. But what if we really do experience thankfulness. I can now see the tree as a storytelling device. Rituals exist because sheer will isn't enough. Because sheer love isn't enough. The pop song I remember from 1998. How to see the things that have become invisible to you. We take each ornament from the box. From its bunched tissue paper. Every house a container for objects awaiting their own dissolution. Today I empty the refrigerator and smell each item before replacing it. Attempting to account for the hours we spend under man-made lights. We wanted to believe in the moral uprightness of bedtime. Your complicated scent-distribution machine. Quotation marks around planning. Wanting to lift and arrange the towering sadnesses contained in the season. I write something about the shortening days and the towering workload. But do you have someone to talk to. I think the phrase I used was *gently suggest*. When the volunteer shift ended without warning. The profound relief of having a place where I was supposed to be in these hours. It's easy to send an email but sometimes this task takes you days. Did you want to see how mortal we are. Left alone to watch birds fly over a neighboring roof. I made a note to watch for images of height and depth. You make a list in order to cross things off it.

THE END

The problem of embodiment had become one protracted crisis. I became a scholar. Confetti on the subway floor. Some light still left across the river outlines a single sharp-edged cloud. Adult onset intellectual vagina. As though time were a substance whose flow you could control. Can you sit down now. Sequins around her sweater cuff. Somewhere John Milton is shouting to his daughters *MILK ME MILK ME*. Not in this case a sexual euphemism. Fashionable sweatpants. Run your finger along the foredge. Most of the graffiti goes by in black and white. I want you to believe that people long dead felt as much as you do. Cried and fucked and looked out a window bored past all feeling. Let's get out of the city. This is perhaps a fiction. Pages of the book so thin her notes bled through. I left the apartment I put on shoes. When you rewrite the same line years later in a new context. The year closing like a trap. You stood clear of the closing doors. Practice dallying. Practice saying it. I find it again. *All the new enclosures*. Writing on my new device. *Excuse me* is a thing that can be said with quiet force. The way corn or soy fields had infected your dreams. Shield and livery of my disappointment. Making perfect. When I was young a stranger's hand was always on my thigh. When I say *fuck discipline* I hope you know what I mean.

THE END

Feelings are so chemical. You've counted five rose bushes still blooming in December. The life you opened up around yourself like a park meadow. What is a week. To oscillate wildly between not believing in discipline and believing it one's only salvation. Let's go look at the river. Book a room for the review. I had hoped to consistently administrate a sensation of inner space and variety. Do you know how to write when you're happy. I wanted to name a literary work that didn't casually describe something like rape. At first it seemed a joke but the title gets more and more apt. Pigeons in the air shaft. You wake up. Move your body around. I wanted to call this *sleep season* or at least *lie on the couch season*. Emotions are so calisthenic. I put a checkmark in the box labeled *Leave Apartment*. The humidifier shushes out a cloud of vapor. Close your eyes and try to see the painting's red drips on a field of canary yellow. I have this grid of activities and emotions. When I accidentally revealed myself as nearly twice my students' age. Do the birds know which way to fly this year. Dress your body up and take it outside. Did you want some new words for this. Don't call us we'll call you. Walking up the path where all the lamps had been broken. Having a body is so boring. I mark it daily as an early warning sign. Where is the line between insatiability and sorrow. Gates and stiles. Make a little room for doubt and it will tear the whole structure down.

THE END

Listening to music an album at a time is an act of formal nostalgia. Let's call this *telling you something you already goddamn know*. Arrive late and blame the trains. To have nothing. To be nothing. Penning an institutional autobiography. We could have a radio show called *Shit-Talk All Your Exes*. Private school public school private school. I've been thinking about the meaning of *impeccable taste*. A purely social member of the film society. Sounds of neighbor TVs coming in from several directions. I thought the footnote was hilarious. *Staring a hole through it all*. The sticky spot on the floor you tested with your feet. Worn seats in the theater. Other solid gold ideas. Wanting to turn yourself inside out. I believe this to be a gender problem but acknowledge the limits of my perspective. Private college state university private university. Three-dollar beers at the bar. If the water is made of prophecy. Nonprofit institution educational institution etcetera. Moment of glare. It's a good time to send a cryptic email. Walk to the co-op for some odd kind of grain. Years since you cried at spending your last cash on bad tomatoes. Sometimes I feel so distant. You were driving through the night and through the corn fields. Never got the brief about so-called safety. It is worse to go out. It is worse to stay in. Sometimes I have the complexion of a motherless child.

THE END

I believe care is a renewable resource. You burrowed into the winter days. As though reading could be that uncharted. Someone painted on the sidewalk *SLIDE THE LIGHT OFF AND GET FREE*. I look right into the ambulance lights. Look how bare my tree is. Who remembers their sentimental education. We habitually underestimate the power of fear. Can you skate along this surface a little more. I feel you wanting to slip between languages. Prop yourself on pillows when you begin to cough. My love sits at a table facing the door. The degree to which your body is visible is the degree to which you are denied anything more. You feared it or you found it ineffactual. All the subway ads trying to make cooking seem like sex. A man tells a woman *it's your world pretty girl*. How the subway passed below the theater as the actor looked down at his feet. When you get quiet the words come. The way you kept turning the book in your hands. That directionless. What if you do your best thinking underground. You forget your wallet and leave the prescription unfilled. She said *I make a space of safety from which to attack*. I do not believe attention is a limitless resource. Call it Human Face Fatigue. Bring a little extinction event over here. Tearing up in the insurance office. I had read the line as *there's no such thing as consent*. This also seemed true. Wanted to keep thinking about Adam and Eve. About Milton's blindness. Can you undo the things you've written. Having read the manifesto of the monstrous typographer. Every choice you make even when you don't know you are choosing. If your primary belief is that you are lucky any moment you are not under attack. It's not like anyone was raised to believe in the UN. Some girls grow into harridans their brothers grow into men. Why don't you tell me what it's like in your body. Yearning toward the hollow center. I came I saw I held your hand.

THE END

Glimpses of the statue through a train window. I wanted things a little less colonized by language. Having refused to believe in safety as a desirable outcome. Yelling in Russian over her daughter's head. Do you believe in the body that dies or in the one you write for yourself. The corporate yoga retreat leader. Salty footstep trail from door to elevator. Was it a choice of time or money. Combine the smooth and gritty and don't neglect the fingernails. Watching the fire escapes for hours. I was nobody's caretaker. I was ready to be destroyed by love. To choose for privation when surrounded with plenty. At the bar with the off-duty beauticians. All the snow blows right into your face. If a history of the majority has ever been possible. Three rolls of paper each wrinkled where you carried them. Enlightenment as export commodity. Sun drifts across the hands of the man in the beautiful cowboy hat. I want to imagine that I could understand most points of view. Sometimes you know what you're doing is *holding court*. His gold-painted face foreshortened by the camera. Theory never or always belonged to you. Knowing how the sugar trade and the tea trade and the textile industry mutually supported exploitation *at home* and *in the colonies*. You believed in the landscape of the lobby. The most-instagrammed party of 2013. The danger of belief in one's magnificence. For a long time instead of thinking I had tastes interests and questions. Plane slowly crossing the unbroken clear sky. Your eye follows the cast iron swags across the molding. If a history of the majority is the problem. Born in the light and inching our way outward. It is good to walk the five extra blocks from the express train. Remembering the thick certainty of young men. First I was a visible body then I was one without surface. Accidentally looked right into the eyes of the man sitting next to you.

THE END

When you were present your voice seemed to come from inside my head. Nothing happens during the day. From the end of this platform to the start of the next stop. What is thought. An essay on false consciousness. I do not know what narratives or feelings I should consider secret. False spring all winter long. What it means to keep arcing toward the unknown. A scrolling sign over the sidewalk reads RECLAIM YOUR MEMORIES. The secrets invariably things I already knew. If books have always been commodities. Who takes all that time in their kitchen. Snow then sun then all the birds in trees. Even disaster takes a break sometimes. My delight in having left the map of traceable relationships. I want to use language to look through but maybe not my own. This speaks less to my personal perceptiveness than to the structure of the psyche. When I clean my desk I feel like a real human for a few days. This means water is a central theme. Having had the luxury of opposing material and psychic comfort. You did not feel an emotional resonance in the landscape. Until someone is masturbating on the train again. When I had boyfriends they often wanted to tell me their secrets. Silhouettes made of subway tiles. It comes back as a series of references I ought to know. Wanting to learn about ambition. You let your eyes dry out a little too much. I do most of my writing in the shower or on the train. Brown water in the humidifier. The glowing wall of glasses frames. When you finished the book something unnameable shifted inside you. Feeling a little evolutionary. Becalmed.

THE END

Unable to sleep I remember the bodies of old lovers. Let's make a policy of this. I was in high school. I was closing ranks. Poetry remains equally impossible. No spot in the room from which you can see the sky while standing. Our paltry business vocabularies. Applying perfume on the street. I think all the time of Rousseau's island of happiness. Turned this sad fate into a moment of perfect pleasure. Adjust your bra strap and stop believing you are dying. Dozing in the library. Once you write them down the words are already out of your control. I go downtown. A pile of damp tissues on my lap. That one spot in your back a container for pain. A night for doing taxes as a couple. So happy to find the ham sandwich. You need a new prescription. I think my husband never used the word. The man on the subway vomits and vomits. How not to retreat into unearned advantage. Never look when someone calls to you. In my head I transformed *sexy thighs* to *sexy fires* to make myself feel better about smiling back. Now remove the tension from your lower jaw. If you want to know how it feels to be here perhaps you should watch the police procedural. When spring gets inside your skin. I wasn't trying to be an important voice of our time. Applying perfume on the subway. Were you fifteen or twenty three or thirty six when your first friend died of natural causes.

THE END

I believe in ages because I've seen time change. Something about the shabbiness of a country not your own. To claim or to be claimed or to be jailed for years without a trial. Not so much Enlightenment's bad dream as its true fulfillment. Every empire comes to an end. The first white blossoms. First daffodils in an allotment outside the train window. You are aware that most of what you do is move your body from one place to another. Smothering coughs at the poetry reading. Reading on the night bus. Approaching the stapled center of the notebook. I hadn't been trying to bear down into relation. Get under the blue sky before clouds cover it up again. Progression of gently qualifying definitive statements and tea in a gold-rimmed cup. Take yourself around the corner to clear your head staring at bas-reliefs. *If you can't drink something warm there's something wrong with it* says a man at the next table. I imagine a day in the not-too-distant future. Indelible chill of almost every bar bathroom. It's easy to get misplaced within a morning. *Stupid boobs* texts Sarah. A scarf as large as a blanket. A slow but drenching rain falls all around the library. Everyone's reception history flags from time to time.

THE END

To register words in writing. A woman tells her son something is *a bit precious* by which she means *not a toy*. I've come to think of this as a Moroccan mirror. Cape envy. Feeling a tug of worldliness I check my hemline in a plate-glass window. Already spring here. All the false daffodils in buttonholes. You put on chapstick and head out into the park. Sunset on the river so unimpressive in the photograph. Can we make this connection every day. I'll stand up as long as there's a place to put my drink. There's poetry and then there's gossip about poetry. *Frosted Foods* reads a sticker peeling from the wall. I thought I heard you hum *we're always touching by underground wires*. Each small thing that might cause your future to pivot. Antlers balanced on the windowsill. Then you're walking along the waterfront with an infant strapped to your chest. All the pots in the window of daffodils or chives. Sometimes you go too far inside for hours or days but sometimes you see and name everything in your vicinity. Seagulls filling up the park. Buy a lemon on the way home. Wake into the bluest sky. I recognize my acquired vocabulary. Titling the review *whose I is this anyway*. There's the threat of rhetorical violence and then there's the threat of real violence. Having to do perhaps with the body in question. She placed my accent in a bar in Soho. Already so far gone into my day. Craning out the window for a glimpse of the famous restaurant. Talk me down before our walk.

THE END

We wished to make an ethical description of our times. This required the simultaneous wearing of two sweaters. Adult women walking by a playground fence. I hadn't kept track of the milestones. Sometimes one must purchase something in order to write while sheltered from the weather. Was it more like a country or more like a neighborhood. You were hungry you were feral. An infant cannot distinguish between various levels of crisis. We wanted to believe we lived in a world made of or made by women. Then I overhear something about *the bourgeois revolution*. I asked if the street was named for the stables it once housed. Two hours to sunset. I wasn't biking on the path. Rain outside falling slow. You had been promised a fireplace and here instead was a life-size wooden greyhound. Something like paying your dues. A day in the marshes. Oh the daffodils and crocuses in the sudden hail. A message appears telling you how much money you've spent on the internet. The world full of its actual shabby objects. I emptied a small packet of salt semi-evenly over my whole plate. The woman by the window talks animatedly to her friend while a baby latches to her breast. In this way the possession of certain resources separates the poet from the not-poet. My apparent agelessness. My only victory.

THE END

Glass leaves on a tiny tree. Did you remember to turn off the heat. At the counter I refused to offer free editorial services. Lacking the basic tools of your trade. I liked the game of ping-pong always happening upstairs. Is it *street harassment* if it starts with *excuse me*. All the women with their thousand-watt smiles. I wanted to reject every kind of knowing. How the word *land* creates an open space for capital to flow through. Life of ongoing small expenditures or my career in small-press poetry. A blunter instrument crying on the tiles. I did not know it was possible to report frottage on the public bus. Obsession is salvation I think walking by Little Baobab. I understand that departure is a kind of luxury. The river flowing southeast all through this part of the poem. You take your body out and feed it. Having made a life of a series of improvisations. On the bus with three drunk teenagers. Do you remember where you left the slippers. We never talk about craft here. The best way to devalue a book is to fill it with poetry. How to use the things you know but cannot cite. It is always only me in here. I liked the taxidermy store flooded with sourceless light. The Red Cross symbol so charmingly painted on brick. I wanted my body to be a deadlier kind of weapon. Burning and burning and nearly half the passengers asleep.

THE END

Having made a form to contain the material life of those days. The heat makes a sound like a distant doorbell. You didn't hear the accident but you heard the sirens coming. Birds outside in the dark heart of the city. How beautiful the letters grow once you have had your coffee. Here's a whole unbroken sky over you. I never know what kind of person to be on the internet. Head of the Buddha at the edge of the counter. We were our own small city then. Joining the society of library poets. The season lodged somewhere in my back. All the owners in the park try to reason with their dogs. Released the psoas muscle while draped over a tree branch. Who opened the window to better see spots of moss on the sill. Light falls from an angle on the overgrown graves. I take this as a sign that all is not yet lost. Became a semi-expert cloud studier. *You know me well & would know me better if I was nigher london.* A woman bent over the man's body still speaking as though he can hear. You set down your things and make note of the table number. Counting footsteps until your wrist begins to vibrate. What you wanted was to watch the postures of the researchers' bodies. We lived in many moments at once. Suddenly forget which river you had been walking by. Two more weeks of making things to precede a week of rest. All this light coming down from a sky you cannot see. Affect breakdown by the fogged bus window. What part of your body won't stop bleeding. So many lanterns hanging over the street.

THE END

Netflix suggests *Dramas That Make John Stamos Feel Emotions*. View out to the harbor. Indeed I did. Actually people everywhere are being fucked by industry and capital and the climate beginning to spiral. I was trying to tell you something about getting closer to the sky. Every city betrays its own internal logic. A sentence structure whose frequency we could not account for. Garden light. A pudding inspiration. I am aware my concerns are prosaic or rather *poetic* in the most jejune way. High-rises not really all that high. Let's hilariously trade expressions for Place Where You Take a Piss. Only an hour and a day late to the reading. Watching the roof slicked in rain. Aesthetics are most of all a problem of epoch and therefore there is no such thing as a cool time traveler. It's true it's mental. Look up. You could open up this wall and still find French doors. Having a canal consciousness. Flowers wrapped in brown paper flow out through the city in all directions. Did you want to be a shelf slowly filling with half-read books. The phone buzzes on the desk. I am angry at myself for watching sitcoms instead of writing about poetry. In the city where I live residence in a tall building may indicate wealth or success. Young people go there. As in the bathroom the toilet the loo. I regret every use of the word *actually* but this one most of all.

THE END

Door to the roof deck chained shut today. Is the canon a grave. Engaging in major descriptive work. The diagnosis that allows your speech to mean or to mend. Placing every battle just where it belongs. Autocorrected to something about ortolans. Why had we saved these tasks to be done in this middling part of our lives. Rolled all around the bed to warm it. You arrive in the middle of an afternoon keeping time so idiosyncratically. *Out of nothing to have come on major weather.* Did we believe in the possibility of ethics and if so upon what grounds. We might understand the self as a useful fiction. The Venn diagram of *what you know* and *what you do*. Cool morning first day of spring. I made a file and named it *Ideas*. Having the qualities of mendacity and viciousness and visionary hope. Sometimes I see you growing older through the screen. In this text I will call upon my administrative voice. Maybe a kind of iron structure to support a conservatory's glass panes. Who else is restless and full of. Figural tendencies get the best of you. I have been watching the dead send greetings to the dead. This is called study. Having abruptly ended the night in the bar and taken a set of blurry photos through a bus window. Walking right out of town. Slowing into the song's compendium. Do you turn back to match a person to the footsteps. Who wanted to be always opening new fronts. Found a pathway by an artificial river. I read to you from a letter sent 200 years ago. Tugging on the legwarmers as I reach the street corner. Passed by on the bus a couple days later. Every name a little too apt. In the name of safety walking out into the street.

THE END

Historically painted women look in mirrors on mansion walls. No privatization no poetry. Dogs with dead deer. Who built a cheaper bridge instead. We have a canon so I can say to you *I'm mad about shooting birds and animals* and you can know what I mean. Vibrating historically to the music. Caring for the bodies of others while remaining to them a stranger. You were twenty and misunderstood you were forty and misunderstood. A known unknown. Hawk Attacking Partridges. Green tiles gleam as the sun goes down behind clouds. Gendered my motion suddenly in a room surrounded by rain. We wanted none of your lifestyle awards. Walking by a canal again. Every joke I could think of came from a masculine canon. *The Toilette of Venus*. Also there have been advances in lighting technology. Who wouldn't want to be a dead poet under these conditions. Stripping away comfort is one way to remove the face. To suddenly find you have transcribed the war. Indeed the scene of predation. I like the shapes of historical asses in paintings. Carrying it all in your stomach. Some factories keep impeccable records. Dogs with dead wolf. Blankness of their rosy faces as though so unseen. I didn't want to parade my fragility or fidelity. A man speaking to abstractions. A single hair hangs from a gilded frame. I was watching the painters watch the women watch themselves.

THE END

Keep your friends close and your ambitions closer. Issuing & returning all day long. Then through the construction each night. What differences might you name in this space. One eyelash growing the wrong way for weeks. Looking at the phone as the buildings get higher. When the clouds blow in again something between a caterpillar and a dove. Footpath through the housing complex. Using my home voice. I was listening to your morning from my afternoon. Riverwalking. Thrilled by the cleverness of some past self. Counted your way down the thoroughfare. No private jokes. The space the museum made for my loneliness. A member of some blue jeans army. Sweeing from a branch. Are you dreaming your parents' yard filled with water from a minigolf fountain. Each rainy afternoon. I did not know any location with intimacy. When you might go around the corner into that filtered light. ATM anxiety. Some interior and mostly immaterial architectures. Like a brightly colored comet in the black screen. Using my away voice. *Glad to have lived to have seen.* You wanted to reach through the page. Nodding intimately to the music. Human scorecard. What I learned about the sky by watching black-and-white films. Poetry as breathing methodology. What did you wish to place adjacent. For a theatrical yawn you came right out into the middle of the day.

THE END

Have you considered trying not to hate anyone. I thought about carrying a museum inside my body. The study center empty and the lights turned off. Impossible to exhaust the set of available paths. Sometimes I was a river sometimes I was sky. Fumbling through currency you almost understand. All for certain species-based distinctions. Did we believe in the existence of the individual or was it the inner Rousseau acting up again. Every single bus all over the city. A feeling that circulates through any space made available to it. A matter of structures and intellectual temperatures. Five skulls carved from human teeth strung on a string. One must consider the mortality of all projects. To form an account in the midst of such riches. Here's another email from someone I hate. Gorged your eyes on the flower bed. Having only the loosest grasp on the absence or presence of sex appeal. I call this *my New England reserve*. When had we all started dying. Wrapped in something between a sweater and a blanket and heading toward the park. The world contains two categories *work* and *distraction*. I had considered the possibility of a warm rose light radiating from my body into every other body in the subway car. I forgot to tell you it isn't all that fun. Working your way into ecosystemic thinking. Heard but did not see a passing airplane through the window.

THE END

In some places money is a weight. A description with doubt built in. *Thanks love ta love thanks*. Fix your eyes on the power lines as the day slips by or you slip through it. The low-lying fields both fenny and blea. Who told me I didn't know the power I had. Water rippling across a glass ceiling. I wanted to be a channel through which intention flowed. Tenderness of the passerby. Held your awareness like a halo around you. Of course we each wished to be a land of exception. Navigating the city by canals. Let me show you that I know what comes next. Anemometer perched on the railing. A yeasty smell accumulates in crevices. Rewards of early rising. You leave the country to align your sentences. Into the fields. Running for the train in tartan leggings. One of the new towns therefore ugly. In an ideal world you would create the archive you need and then turn to it. Some kind of reunion. Hold each clothing item up to the camera. I said *cost* but you heard *weight*. Interrupted rhythm. Fur ruff. To believe money is materialized intention is to court a social despair. The vanity of a purposely bad haircut. My love my shining device held before the face. How does your voice reach the portals of my ears. Some places money is a ghost. Houses at night as you head down the block. All stations and flashing lights. Not that I didn't want to flow like water. *Who's going to look after the dragons* she said.

THE END

My friend the drunk teenager disappears at the station threshhold. Light breeze on leaves growing over the fence. Like all of human history. I mean really literally only pop music for years. Having been like *a double quarto sheet which has become unstitched and separated from a larger volume*. Because I am always in a city. A kind of gathering dusk. Stepped into the crypt sound installation. Womb color morning. Sun on roof tiles. Why does everyone love carpets so much. Presses and writers and favorite streets we all keep in our small notebooks. Or I am always on a train. *Now you'll regret that white jacket* I joke under the overpass. Victorian cutouts in a high window. My gender or my genre. I came I saw I bought a beer. The labor of an army of long-dead framers. Night out with the poets again. Laundry day again. Hammering sound like a bird's flapping wing. Having become a sort of walking travelogue. The men so abstract and the women so pictorial and modest. Your face hard to remember without a real effort. Maybe this is what sends you north. Let us envision floating down the river where it's narrow and overgrown with trees. I start at the edges and slowly fill in the middle. Framed by capital. The children are building a Lego boat again. The problem I often think is that I am one thousand years old. Trading recommendations all over town. Her sweater covered in buttons *ten minutes from the sea*.

THE END

Here is the steeple. I wish to speak on behalf of My Community. Watch your body invitationing as though suspended from above. I came in dragging all my stupid luck. So moved by his illegible handwriting by his testing of the pen. At this table some of us can move freely while some of us possess fewer options. I wanted to know how literature might form a response to our various crises. The afternoon filling up with doubt. How lonely do we think a cloud gets up there passing through the sky and through its friends. You go to lie down in the strange-smelling room. Productive fiction of the lost first love. What you saw from the top of the Necropolis just a city just another palmed over morning. Yet we still wish to laugh together over dinner. Is literacy's historical frat-status the material of a good or a bad joke. Depends how fast the light changes. The thing was I read the footnote and I knew she was asleep when kissed. Flapping tarp. Diagnostic consensus might be that I had been a pretty woman once. Trailing through weeds. If Britney can get through 2007 he told me. Because I was a Man of Taste. Drag yourself out of bed for a dinner party in a new city. The only thing that can be said is I am sorry you cannot return to your country. Daffodils still blooming in a low spot in the marsh. It is after all a real skill you're learning. Voices in the hallway. Do you choose the poet's birthplace or his grave. Women my age have affairs in all the novels. Rushing down the slope on the other side of intention. I am a patroness of the arts I give to all the kickstarters. Productive fiction of the last love. Forecasted light rain in the evening. I am angry at the world but I am not angry at you.

THE END

Coal smoke like a time machine. We were young we were breaking. Past the skate park the train pulls *out of my knowledge*. I believed this might become my actual life. To see with a thrill children playing without a parent in sight. Unidentified birdsong as all birdsong is to me. Uncertain the conditions of our lives have permitted us to become fully human. Had you called yourself the transcendental surplus. The harbor so smooth today. The tide coming in. Partly this is a string of refusals. Each poem crossed out as it is copied. How did we all know what a walk looked like when you made it into words. Blades at the wind power plant turning slowly in the distance. Each of us has helped to make life unlivable for people we loved and for people unknown to us. A syntax beats inside the body. This is one of the forms. The roadwork sign bearing your initials. As if all we wanted was to catch a cloud's reflection in the surface of a puddle or pool. I forget to remove the heavy felt sleeve and carry it all about the island's edge. Not having expected this restlessness to go on and on. You fell into situations. You *grew as a person* and this made you opportunistic and this made you cold. Small chips of diamond. Abrupt edge of a pond. Did you want to be the wrong kind of person to be something other than recognizable. Beset with many claspers. Ducking down by the tidepool.

THE END

I worry that I have not found a space for joy in these poems. To be a bridal path or to be a warpath. Two castles an hour. Hello darling. Would have preferred to find a path but instead I found a gate. I spent money to make this space of silence and then I leaned into it. The tide is going out. The next step is always to bring someone in. The field full of something on the other side of sadness. I think you'd call this substance *time*. Startled again by starlings in a hedge. Fake it or naked. One kind of poem for when you are alone and this is the end every time. So thirsty for years. You were handsome you were pretty you were counting 123. To traipse through the field that was not yet houses. Does your disciplinary inner voice speak in the second person. Money in money out. Was it made of wood from the beloved poet's deathbed. Having taken myself for a walk I wonder about the dialogic form. I had entered my decadent phase which was university funded and far from home. Starting with hot water and slowly adding the cold. The stone told you lovingly that one day everyone you know will have been dead for millennia. Yes and back again. I meant that I was capable of either love or song. Wanting to know where humor ends and joy begins. Two round rocks each cracked down the middle. Did you think that language was your private playground. Made a spell to invite our ghosts in. Avoid eye contact with birds. The ways in which my family is a foreign land might tempt me to think I can know your life. I wanted to leave a mark on language. I wanted to mark it with my teeth.

THE END

As though a giant scale descended from the sky with justice on one side and aesthetics on the other. Autocorrected *flâneurs* to *flameouts*. This said David is the effect of late capital. Not teleology just change. Irregular train service. Passenger jets passing over the downs. Can we all stop talking about the impoverishment of the scholar. Walked down the street muttering a spell against satisfaction. Who had seen the saddest ending of a night out on the tiles. A book or a magazine beckoned you from the window. Swaying through blooms on the second story of a bus. The children naked running up and down the stairs. It seemed that I had been lying about the weather. I don't know. Yes and no. Let us read like enemy agents in the heart of civilization. A familiar awning lights up the screen. From the corner of my eye the card read *You Are My Lobster*. Hashtag wealldiealone. Perhaps it was the affect of late capital. I guess I wanted us to define terms. Tonight you are a light box on my lap my love. Poverty not the same thing as lack of wealth. Calendared your sorrow meaning burnished it to make it shine. Fox on the front walk. The danger of our times was no one stood by the ocean watching it warm. Not that things were fine before the Enlightenment. Hand-me-down transit systems of the north. A woman swimming from a dark room into a window's rectangle of light. Because believing in a better world isn't incompatible with living in this one. I fell asleep at the gates and let everything through.

THE END

Wanting to live at the hem of law or capital. My unremarked body winds through the crowd. Who had gone like underwater. Heterosexual monogamy as economic in origin. Let us enumerate our luck to decide what we owe to the public sphere. Passing by the Church of Wonderful God. We used to make things in this space but now we make feelings and ideas. Landscape paining. Luxury apartments all around the stadium. Mother and infant as an intimacy intruded obscenely on the space of intellectual labor. On a train with a paper towel shoved in my underwear. Having found the precipice you tumble down the far side. Hello friend I do not yet know. Could you be this little green cloth I keep to rub raindrops and oils from my glasses. To be a signal problem. How to make that daily tenderness human. *The wandering hands of civic engagement* I wrote as a joke with perhaps a dark underside. One problem of a revolution is where to put the feces that have arrived in the public square. Some places are less truly places than others he said. Patched existence under the beam of excess. I wanted to think about the language of *owing* as applied to our relationships. The same climate the same businesses. Do sexualities connote a disposition toward or away from the movement of capital. Paper dissolving in homemade ink. Over the beautiful floodplain.

THE END

I learned to protect myself by smiling. Flew up and down as though stitching field to sky. Blazing fields of rape across the southern countryside. Where I've been living. Or maybe born this way. What is to be said about this slip in landscape vocabulary. Blue warehouse wall fills the window like an abrupt new sky. Were you nineteen on a park bench or twenty in a cul-de-sac. Every river is the same river. Because to lie on the ground means to neither see nor be seen within the human world. Fine line between poacher and poet. Nina writes of the fight or flight feeling filling her body and many of us say *yes me too*. To be poor is to be a crime against property. Train by the horse reclining in a patched blanket. Itchy trigger tongue saying and saying it. Three birds in the stubbly field. What words you keep from your mouth but sob around the edges on a Greyhound months later. Were you fifteen in a car. Coming into major fields. Is to desire or not to desire a crime against safety. I meant the plant not the action. In the South I learned to say *aren't you sweet* and floated blissfully up to the ceiling. To resist the erotics of anger and fear. To name your love and let it fly away. Were you twenty in another country home late from the bar. Because this kind of knowing is both hammer and nail. The way sunlight touches you all over and you are glad. Every thing blooming into the present. Were you younger much younger and were you at home. Can I name you and name you and name us into a new world. Shaken at the seminar by sourceless rage. Walking to a phone booth at night to call a friend. *Even temperate skies were lined with the sublime.*

THE END

Flanked by figures of Fame and Death. Did you use up all your energy being loved by strangers. Flashpoints along the building's skeleton. Turning weather into value. I found I wanted to do the work that took most from me. Acquired an ache. By the side of the path holding her clearly broken wrist. Strange bone-itch of an hour on cold metal chairs. Possibility of changing hearts or of speech across a river. *The site extends for miles*. Somehow the afternoon flits away. Wanting to stand in the center of your voice. Something not quite research. There is a future in which I learn how to drive. April marked by hail dully hitting wet stones. Who else had come from the theatre and how had their bodies changed during the show. How *lowland* resists immediate identification until you have seen its opposite. Wanting to imagine a world in which *safety* is emptied of its rhetorical power. Engaged in an anti-publication process. *To him a sheep was a machine for turning grass into mutton*. Whether to call this thing I live within *material* or *time*. In which I learn to drive you away. Gesturing a space towards voices of greater urgency. But I mean what if a body is only matter. Exhaustion and a vague desire for sitcoms. What does this music drown out besides the clatter of money turning back into time. This is how I know the difference between love in the body and love online. *This time I'm telling you*.

THE END

The building settled & the windowframe widened until the glass could be easily pushed aside. In summer the body even more permeable. Hotel room night again. Experiments in fearlessness in making a new world each time. While washing dishes I ranked my traitorous desires. You were a liquid you were a thought. *To remember the ship and the horse upon the glittering sea.* A five dollar umbrella for each rainstorm that caught you out. What if noticing is your skill. Writing under duress and underground. Old fruit in the fridge. As in *to endure*. Having reached orgasm primarily through acts of late-morning frottage. A place to lie down in the grass. No birth *ex nihilo*. No bridge to connect or divide. The woman says *people these days are taking it to the level of the demonic*. Some lost season coming in through the window. Up the stairs and into the sunlight. To betray my race my nation my family my gender my species. Is it possible to disagree with this prognosis. Having overpaid for the strawberries. To be loved for one's ethics. Your feet on the tunnel floor crossing under the river. Then something like a gunshot. We enter the artificially heated room and our skin starts prickling. Wastebasket full of expired painkillers. Underline the category *at risk*. I was lodged under the skin. I caught in the throat. You came you saw the city disappeared.

THE END

Wandered the summer night like capital. Was Hobbes describing war as a kind of weather. I lacked the immediacy of a face. Because sanctuary. What might make you want to believe. I mean like a cloud made manifest over time. Teetering along an edge of despair but witnessing nevertheless. Heard you singing along to Lauryn Hill by the sun-cleaved plate glass. Being here with me in morning and in night. Appearance of softness in the fresh tar patches. We kept time each summer by acts of violence dispersed through the air. Please put on your owl eye mask. Moving like sound through the darkening park. Yes I am the world's greatest drummer. The initials of a long-dead dictator. We crossed the bridge by accident and we kept driving. In the bar speaking the names of defunct publications. What I mean is made of many migrant desires. Because the blank page is never really blank. Because boats overturn in many seas. Not the man himself but who shaped the vista centuries before. Hearts and minds. Have you seen the subway ad for our city's exceptional drinking water. Empire trigger sequenced in a dance song. In the back of a taxi scrolling through time. Wanting to know your stance on nations. Looked up the poetry reading but found the massacre instead. Rerouted over a hill onto the street of mansions. I meant not just no borders but no skin. Utopia as horror movie is what I think Arendt would say. Some words catch at you in the shower. Another vigil. It wasn't all rosebushes and boarded-up houses. It was good lying next to you but your snoring kept me awake. The problem was for one a belief in earthly salvation. A rash prickling the skin inside my elbows. Garment care as self-making.

THE END

Around the patio table and below the full moon. I overwrote your atmospherics into a somber key. *Contract what. Covenant what.* Thanks for leaving your gym clothes outside today. Overtaken on the path again. The skin of my face cracked and peeling. Like how do we survive. In a species sense. The season in which we play *firecracker or gunshot*. You track the insufficiency of your sleep across the week's spreadsheet. The problem with this kind of scholarship is that it's always passing through. Two kids shot halfway across town for being Muslim are sleeping in their hospital beds. Eyes on the river. Brush your hem on this enormous cockroach belly up on the sidewalk. Who mothers. Naming our invisible labors. The easy irony of my inability to stop watching televised addiction dramas. Walking through the park again. Removed to high country or breezing through airport security. Did we make a new kind of day. It's hard to tell when you're going to reach the real shit. Little spots on the windscreen. Sweating along the river. A parade often makes me tear up. Our bodies as machines producing various liquids and unguents. Should have yelled *I LOVE YOU ALL* to the Dykes on Bikes. Thinking of you at your citizenship appointment. The four-year-old wakes me with a lion's roar at my bedside and I stumble down the stairs. Thinking of the bodies each century piles up. Insensate to the sun. There's whiskey in the jar.

THE END

If empire were a frame would you hold it up. You'll find these notes next year in the pile of untouched manuscripts. Flipping backward and forward through historical time. The human body so diegetic. Find and use all the scraps. I wanted to lead the class through a bygone revolution. Every night tearing at the edge of private utterance. Made a plan in which walking is the polestar. A wolf on a waterslide on a phone screen in bed. You write in a notebook *how to conquer*. Slivers of light around the edge of the curtain. Give yourself a day off and a whole week passes. Who thinks right while lying down. A mysterious envelope arrives from the archive. Thinking morning doing afternoon. The task is to put your body in front of other bodies. I saw them holding hands by the faculty housing. Don't say you're sorry. One trail of cloud. We were *getting into silence* all that summer. *I cannot paint what then I was*. Intimacy as cost-benefit analysis. I found the map of bookstores after I left the city. Had there been a protest while we were in the movie theater. Time to get up but the body rebels. My mental architecture more of an open plan. Did I ask you to help with the things I needed help with. Stood politely around the empty seats inside an all-over ache. We wanted to say *that's not my canon*. Likewise for all the secrets of a happy marriage. I mean the light was everywhere. Hand-tracing the course of the river. Spots of illegibility scattered across the novels. Fell so hard on the ice I peed a little on impact. Fissures opening in the group each week. Weaving between barricades on the way to the subway. Over the years a person will grow self-referential. But could you still be of another place or time. From the outside they appeared as two separate restaurants. Did you return the library books. Did you buy the paper. Feeling makes a rhythm and that rhythm becomes a season. Who held up the frame & who looked around its edges.

THE END

A voice from somewhere says *produce produce*. Darker outline of the waterstain on the ceiling. The year gets away from you. At night I lie on the blue couch to read from the pile of pale blue books. Epochal rise in parts per million and anthrax near the pole. The author photo stuck in time while the writer ages away from it. Aching rationality and rage. *Another round* we cry triumphantly. Thinking we already have enough friends. That living you did on the page or in the box of the lighted screen. Old-timey soundtrack of typewriter noises. Every day I think about taking our pillows to the laundromat. Liking this sunset I saw through the phone. I wanted to make things that existed in time not space. Can you describe your pain using this one-to-ten scale. Then see a whole self hurtling toward an extinction. Twinge in the knee as you rise from your chair. I envision a future in which we're already taking a bottle up to the rooftop. Rain comes down like a curtain again. Metric tonnages. Over the counter and under the stars. In my twenties I too believed people learned from their mistakes. Another death and another one reach you through the screen. My body is getting older so I take it to the room of music. When you walked through the last month in your mind. Always the smudge of forehead grease on the train window. The typewriter. The sewing machine. Christmas stockings on the wall in the beginning of August. The dark cave of your mouth or of your living room. Clustered around the statue holding up their devices. Bleeding for two days after the procedure. Did you line up the books and dream about reading your way across. Every single tiny act against entropy.

THE END

Making a policy of quantity not quality. Our daily walk to the train. Run your eyes all over these pages. As though storms. Porcelain-sick. We call these behaviors *upkeep*. To fill the home with living things or with sheets and sheets of paper. I grew vigilant in my shame. Something real was shaking us down. I raised the monitor to eye level and steered clear of the couch. Branches whipping in the wind and rain. A jam inside. When women weren't allowed to cross the university lawn. What kind of argument does the seaside painting make. Time passes. Our daily filing task. Is it still plagiarism if everyone knows. The afternoon a brown fog undoing her stockings. Inside a poem I found a tinned dinner. Icy breeze from inside the museum. Remove the drawer from the desk and set it on the other side of the room. Aching hip before bedtime. Learning to believe in *always* and *never*. Blue dye where my palms brush against my new jeans. The city like an oven boiling off a plate of stagnant water. A strange man speaks to me so I put on a cardigan. Writing back to the poets of another age. A person as a set of questions strung through time. To have a voice but no certainty about how or when to use it. The park full of people and pigeonshit. Why give a name to periods like these. In the back seat fighting nausea. Ancient soda bottle full of dried flowers on the table. The river was a tent under which we gathered to speak. We were throwing a party and everyone was invited.

THE END

The river made me do it. A seducer's journal or a film of drugs and sex. I said *storytime* because the summer lulled. Room of beautiful and finite bodies. Mysterious burn mark six feet up the wall. To be a poet at any given moment in history. *The bitter pill needed gilding.* Swimming into a deep street sorrow. I worry that my interests make me unbearable. Including readings emotions and current events. The clouds looked like they'd been drawn on the sky by a toddler with dull sidewalk chalk. Which is to say marked time. A day in which you get over. Thinking of you by the *Wet Trash* sign. Now this is what your face will be like. Only half-joking we typed GOSSIP HAS VALUE. Was it a question of the abducted hip seizing. An accent mistaken for something born not made. Divorced from the form. I loved the lack of future in old photos. Leaving the notebook in public view. I believed in the method but not in the genre. Burning all forms always. Some music comes loose from its moment and drifts through subsequent decades. Knuckles aching and scratches on the wood. Night leaves smudges all over your glasses. Some wind moving through. Having made a method for presenting or being present. Dropping away from what people call a world. We stumbled back from the boat into the coming season. Burnt through words. Diving off the dam. What can be seen from the window and what comes inside your body. Alone at my desk I whisper *sing to me.*

THE END

A person puts a second person inside a third person. *An elegant offense.* We call this the mystery of life. Saxophone punching up through the airspace above the park. Having misjudged an air of cultivated abandonment as bohemian faithfulness to the cause. Like a train skipping stations. Renewing the polis. No one stops being their shitty self. I believed the men I loved wished like me to have and to be nothing. Sick maw. Beautiful condensery of rage. I mean a body's not such a thing. The crowd's terribleness comes from inside you. Shrink-wrapped curbstones all the way home. Encountered you as mouthfeel. And here's night again. A patch of gender in the class-space. A city made of gorgeous cursives and beams of light. I wanted to tell them *after this it is possible everything might be ok*. Visiting the Williamsburg high-rise. Out of the still-wild zones by the river. Paper crimes. Who imagined being judged as hopelessly bourgeois. To be traveling south and then traveling southerner. Might I be your night. No one wants to say *wait a decade and you'll know what I mean*. The punchline was his linen pants. After the ice my knees rattled like jars of pennies or buttons.

THE END

He said *now people know Nina Simone because of the documentary*. Wanting a theory of knowledge that could account for desire and for histories of more than a few years. Which is to say each song as it entered your consciousness. Continuous diffident present. This is again a language problem. I had agreed to speak against safety in a room of my peers. Sounds of late morning coming in from all directions. Glad I had dressed myself again. Having been paid $17 an hour and health insurance to perform excitement in emails. Underleveraged as the candidate says. Those roaches in the kitchen again. On the desk I watch the book spine skyline reshape daily. Each span of meandered hours. What the seasons made your skin into. The more I give my community the more it wants. What recourse to living in the animal kingdom. Every day a list of tasks that might be put on pause when an old friend comes unexpectedly to town. We had the same haircut but it didn't mean we were the same. Shy smiles of the boys who work in the bookstore. As though time had agreed to move this slow. Plotting a library of the future or the light of another coast. The bridge foreshortened as you crossed it.

THE END

A friend punched in the face on a subway platform by a man she ignored too well. What sky I wanted to say. I filled the refrigerator with food to express my love. Dissolved into sunlight. No connection between *hymn* and *hum*. A helicopter swoops in close. Watching *Desk Set* to stay awake for the phone call. The search bar suggests the name of a man killed by police last week. Finding an empty restaurant on the first cold night. Were you sending your love through a series of tubes. Kids in the airshaft mark a new season. As though the last three days had become a portal to Glasgow 1997. Trading up for the brighter room. The brightening noon. No connection between *hymn* and *hymen*. At the end of each night to say *that was a good night*. Powers of speech. Powers of horror. Have we imagined these songs of matriarchy. Waking into another orange sky. Rechecking the *Online Etymology Dictionary*. I made a panic soundtrack. I got right into bed. Weighted into some new gentleness. A friend of friends killed by her roommate. Leaves browning into the streets. Remembering an old anger I am suddenly in its center again. Hey goddess. Who were these people who reported once having felt safe. Who metabolized the nation as a kind of carapace. Let's check the polls again to give a name to our unease. Like every month we waned a little toward the future.

THE END

Let this be an abject lesson. Also laughter arrives in the street. We were throwing names around as though they weighed something. Not until the shark emerges wholly can we see its clumsy construction or the machinery moving below the flesh. Rain becomes stoic. Something you know is suddenly made to appear useful. Enameled nails clicking against the table. In the country shit becomes fertilizer. Words had been spoken into the mediating organs. Here the air above the entire city. A cosmetic or cosmogonic effect. Looking for a spot in the wall to anchor to. Two women speak loudly in the library in a foreign language. The candidate's mouth was everywhere. Also a schedule of guided walks. Having made that century a lens to clarify or to drive sunlight into scorching. Absentee from the polis. Truant of capital. Some stray notes from a nearby piano. Motions of the incoming tide turned to a haze by the film's long exposure. Conditions of the real formed an impediment to sleep. Every two seconds another story. In the city moving through zones of urine smells and zones free of such smells. Meanwhile marooned in my cleverness I brewed a catastrophic amount of Earl Grey. How high could we count before time ran out forever. Bubbles rising in the glass. Shades pulled down at the end of the school day as in a plane landed in a sunny afternoon. The ship of reason sinks endlessly in an icy and distant sea.

THE END

In the bath suddenly whelmed by an idea or plan of action. Also possessing generational skills. For example an inclination toward the form of the experiment. When I said *I have written these sentences* I meant *many of these sentences have been encountered by my ears or eyes*. Outside the window a child cries. An ethnographic experience of hand skills and head skills. I said *because language moves through you at speed*. Like a nest in its relation to sky. Chainsaw season. Dissenting from the notion of craft. In the home the world falls away and so must be narrated quickly on entry. The way science permeated my days. The postures of young people who are dutiful but bored. Beating a rug on the fire escape. I had taken to performing my lack of expertise. Perhaps the need for a wife is always topical. Touching the doorframes as you pass through. I may have spoken some unattributed sentences. To do one's thinking in public and in a body. For example a tendency to forget one's birth year. This opens a small gap that may undermine certain structures. Some quelling preoccupations seem to descend while others seem to arise. Bollywood music from the other room. Its father resoundingly tells it to stop running. Having taken up a formal interest in gossip. I didn't show the video because I found it distracting and because a nervousness permeated my body. Who had written those words. Full moon in Aires. Sun lightening the street and slowly darkening it without ever appearing visibly through the window. Because the violence came from everywhere without warning.

THE END

Returning home weighted by a day of disobedience. Small nick in the window glass. *But* I said *let's talk about our knees.* How the flowers on the windowsill bowed their little heads. White-painted trim both ornate and incomplete. Roar of the train's passage through the open window. Like how dancing suddenly opens a roaring well inside you. The 8.5" by 11" sheet a purely contingent form through which the world is known. The plastic wineglasses melted a tinge off from round. Here was my surrealist syntax again. Still we parted on the street with an inaudible but easily parsed sign. A small number of postures available to the life of the mind. Searched for a way to peel apart the labor of making gender from that of making race or class. Mostly I walked. Like how the boyfriend's blazer made me feel that lip gloss might be required. Let us call this an incommodious movement. But pleasure now may not always mean pain later. Uneven darkness of the skirt at the raincoat's edge. Then the sky cracked open into a final gasp of summer. Drawn in bitters into the egg-white foam. Online tutorials may play a role in this. Church bells come from no discernible direction and there's a cheerful breeze in the one tree you can see. The satire so thick even I could recognize it. Making another mark on the post-it note for each future you foreclose. But isn't this where you want to get off. Stepped through time at a more or less dignified pace. Every day is today while it's happening. Every yesterday recedes from view.

THE END

I don't have feelings about the hyphenation of self-transcendence. Transit sounds from distant highways. Instead we gave rhetorical powers to the climate. Black smoke billows behind the water tank. Think of the city as a set of facial practices collaboratively scripted by a few million people. In which *keeping on the sunny side* becomes a guiding navigational principle. Some crystals dangling from a wall sconce in an empty room. Preserved this silence by knowing when to depart. A bird's flight reflected in the desk's glass top. Did your eye carry a line drawing of a cell performing photosynthesis. I feared the unmoving feet in the bathroom stall might be attached to a no-longer-living body. Midday clouds strangely purpled over the park. How the world of the social buzzes and twangs. Named the neighborhoods of a foreign city with more or less basic competence. Your aura a bright blur greening at the lower left. What is the emoji for *I feel so used*. Today I traveled to mitigate the intrusion of seasonal tiredness. We might call this seeking a new kind of sustenance. Like when the wind died down in the Black Hills. New clouds passing over the old television aerial. I advanced a thesis into the brightly lit space. The man on the train gently rustles his plastic bag. *But also* she said *at times an inexplicable joy*. Speaking back to plant matter. Which is to say your mind kept moving while your body remained in the chair. The tears they had forgotten just resting on the face. Call it a radicalization and scan the sky for drones. In this way you became a being essentially tied to this ecosystem.

THE END

In this moment I want to hold my commitment to sincerity at a skeptical distance. Smell of chicken soup spilling through the train car. The weather warms and cools but Halloween stretches on. Notation and method. How the swelling seemed to pass to the adjacent finger. The safety from predators some landscapes provide. You locate yourself by the jingling entering your left ear. Pleasure in a bar snug. A little in love with the failed notion of privacy. We wished to explore how leaving for the country would shift our perception of time. Hail comes down as we lie in the performing bed. I was protected by a refusal to name some forms of suffering. The sad drugged life of a koala. Boots thudding behind you dare a look back through the empty passageway. As though a large branch fell on the roof and dragged itself rapidly back along the train. Some languorous spelling opened up a new space in the afternoon. Sitting on slightly damp grass an even distance between two men sleeping wrapped in blankets. A woman in a top hat passes by slowly holding an enormous bouquet of roses. What I mean is the presence of necessity at the heart of the most laboriously attained pastoral. Not to build a reputation in a time of mass emotion. Instead I made my economic life a kind of architectural shadow work. Touch up the fingernails with a slash of opposing color. Here is where you might stand between cars to photograph the nocturnal city.

THE END

Mostly as a poet I have studied my own failure. Let us say the social is a black box problem. Pile of mismatched socks bleaching on the windowsill. The political space between what has been promised and what may be possible. All along the flooded cracks. Having desired an editor to rest in the mouth like a bowerbird. One eye on protests under a wider sky. Every night to re-enter the room of ambient weightlessness. Another misapplication of *catastrophe* to purely personal problems. The man across the train suddenly vomits into his own lap. We wanted to know what *mixtape* meant to the current generation. We came to see these cyclical performances of emotion as a kind of call and response. Laughing out loud in a sudden burst. As a scholar I would call this *an affordance of the genre*. Unable to refrain from giving unsolicited advice via email. As though every problem is solvable with the correct application of design software. Wearing into something like comfort. Having overperformed the gestures of belonging so that they exceeded every frame. All the systems invisible to the bulk of their participants. First and foremost the forms of art song. Sovereignty always ripe for replacement by market demand. The classroom fills and empties at hourly intervals. As a daughter and wife I claim an interest in a range of obsolete affects. Hanging over the box of photographs. No one wants to think of the kitchen as a site of interspecies collaboration. Once we liberated the temporal markers we simply vanished from the room.

THE END

A woman on the street is told *not to drink too much from sadness*. Because every beginning is also an end. Following the *hot and panicky money* across the screen. Were you a need or a desire. A decade in the technology of print lodges in my dominant shoulder. Strained to watch his chest filling with air. No turning back. Hands shaking on the plane. The end I documented was not one I had believed. Because there is no such thing as *mankind*. Time at both the human and the historic scales. Matt writes of the fear in rural bars at night. Then smoking returns to common practice. Replace allies with accomplices. In this way every body acts as a lens on the political. Yet I found the presence of a crank invariably soothing. Synthesized voices from the far room. Let us furiously dogear every one of these days. Man on the street says *now* we're *disenfranchised*. No new world. I believed there was a limit to the obsolete skills a body might absorb. Let us not forget the time of stones. When I hadn't yet looked at every white man with suspicion. Did you grow accustomed to the way your hands hung at your sides. She said *I didn't think you would still be here*. Just walking around gingerly in the broken world. Because there are no tears in revolution. There is some comfort in the belief of continuation. Craft as a basically absorbent relation to time. But that was then etc. How to take the love you've learned and turn it toward the dying. A symphony composed for music box and laptop. Some printers invent a series of dance moves to evade further deterioration. *This oracle whose voice is almost indistinguishable from the rumble of history.*

THE END

Hours of busy signals. We urgently needed to know what it felt like to live in history. A squirrel runs by with a nut in its mouth. The tour guide at Versailles had said *belief in Rousseau made him unable to govern*. To abandon the symbols or to flood them with meanings. In the restaurant eavesdropping on the famous chef. Morning made a seam in the new weather. While shaving I imagine a feminist state of nature. Let us ask again whether children are *hopes for the future or unwilling victims*. Returning to a series of fictional flags. Clouds to denote the unknown or otherworldly. Who was it that urged you *to wait and see*. Or was it *to garden*. Chandeliers hang over the organizing meeting. The new weather was made of cops or was one in which brave cops stood between you and something worse. These few snowflakes might be missed by a casual observer. Had I really spoken only a month prior. Lemonade seas. We got off one stop past enlightenment and walked the rest of the way. Still time to invent a new term. Around the conference table a move from feeling to concrete actions. Then a feather lands on the neighboring roof. Old patterns suddenly recur as showtime crosses the river again. I texted a few small moments of the day across the country to you.

THE END

When you reached the end you wanted to lie down but had to keep or to start fighting. Laundromat or temple. We took up residence in an online petition. She said it's been years since we could pretend this crisis has an end. Becca and I talk again about talking about the book. A little victory sweeps through our wires. I had been meditating on the card that reads *meritmeritmerit*. Fumigated the kitchen with a spray made of peppermint and wintergreen oils. Smoke gets in your lungs. A methodology for resisting everything. Together we arrived at the solution of unarmed police and unarmed populace. This made the body into a new kind of law. In light of the new country morning ached out of bed. Place the Christmas tree in the laundry cart. Fear entering the kitchen. How to show the long span of continuous planetary time as it relates to the unrolling catastrophe of any current century. All the snows elsewhere. Pain of watching arrested moments before the break. Instead a series of infinite crescendos. The flowers dead but still saturated with color. Pull back the curtains on another field of gray. Coming to Jesus may not take away your anger. Some lies no longer need to be told. Distant wind chimes carried across a momentary lull until the traffic and sirens again take up their roles. Maria wrote *the mode of this passage is irony not hope*. Driving across the prairie like driving across the moon. What if everything counts. Limning some sketched republic. How to balance the absence of time for despair with the need to laugh bitterly and often.

THE END

Dinner parties continue. A matter of returning the critique to the grounds from which it sprung. Perched on the very edge of the subway seat. I had lived in a body which stiffened and aged. Like a new fear of war blown through. Vaulted glass. Crowded out by things mutely breathing. Of course rain forms a vehicle for time travel. Clear water between. Our first mistake was allowing snow to stand for uniqueness rather than collectivity. What has now become necessary to tell loved ones. Turn off your eyes for an hour. Cleaning out the fridge becomes a utopian practice. We call this an arcade. Of course there is always more to read on past totalitarianisms and climates. The problem was that I could not name a single place where my ashes might be scattered. Still made a passageway from the living room to 1996 and then sent my love down. Drooped over the desk. The way snow masses and melts and leaves a world of thawing dogshit behind. Clutter in the schoolroom window. Not all experiments carry an equal chance of failure. Pigeons in the plaza wheel and wheel.

THE END

I get a haircut to mark my dissent. Tree lights fade brighten and blink. On the screen the beautiful suit of the assassin. Made a white room breathe audibly. Living in and for meatspace. Little snows accumulate. We called this *going home*. Honey light on evening faces. Floor pieced together from large slabs of plywood. I wanted to channel some sobriety through our held hands. All the cars along the avenue gritted in winter silt. Pleasure becomes a responsibility. Because you were given a set of choices and buoyed by tiny lucks. Who made it out in the brief ceasefire. Who came back bearing greenery. To lie down inside the rhythm of your sleeping breath. New survival techniques fly south. I write in the hope that the bitterness of the final years may be allayed or staved. Each tree branch swings and invisibly tugs its fellows. *Because now our job is to protect each other.* Not to lean against the decorative features. Piled into a taxi in a luxurious afternoon. How to love you without fulfilling your desires. What conditions end quickly like a curtain dropping. Little ice shattered by the curb. I urgently needed not to pass. Or a hobby like skiing. If you don't receive money you may call your labor unalienated. Resting the heavy bag for just a moment on the stair. A man sleeps on the station floor in loving embrace with a pit bull. I consider a muskrat skull as a gift to my love. The year slipping along its rails. To build a face from the materials of history. We found a space in the mouth for a new kind of laughter. I believed I could lie curled inside the giant disco ball. *We did not file a police report because we do not trust the police.*

THE END

This was an affective prehistory of the crisis. Little glints of light from LA MEXICANA GROCERY. A white phone in my white hand camera rolling at the first sign of trouble. All bodies leak. Sadness registers as a lag in the machinery. The sky turns briefly and improbably blue. We were either a kind of weather or else a kind of time. A lack of physical discipline means suffering continues unabated. Blue light over the PIONEERS AND SOLDIERS CEMETERY. Planes arc overhead while history seems to plunge. A dense gray cloud hovers on the mountain. Blood in the nose persists. The canal turns left near a circular structure and carries you along the path. On the wall a woman holds a large white lotus and a machine gun. Mostly I became a series of gestures. What next generation. Black spines of books build a black block in vision. Who lit a candle for the electors. You asked for a bathrobe and were given the bathrobe of your dead father. Fibers buried in the nail polish. The studio disarticulated and moved a hundred feet north. As though easy journey from his deathbed were possible. Unmade by uncertainty and the theatrical rollout of the new order. The way a body might sex or become sexed. Up the elevator and down the stairs.

THE END

Hello to the handsome young man in his blue apron. Meanwhile the rain picks up. We learn from Congress that the revolution begins after midnight. One physiotherapist is a dancer while the other one lifts weights. Some sounds echo through your interior spaces. On the bridge a blue and a red light blink and blink. Let us say that we live in bodies and that these bodies live in time. Some blackened leaves just hanging there. Against sunset. What I mean is uninterrupted. Imagine *a room that has perfect scale*. Circulating all night through our bodies. Institutions you believe in or simply believe. Marvelous birds. Slowly rising and falling with a wobbling motion within a landscape of barges and cargo trains. Because joy arrives with a political undertow. The shape of each finger describable as a tightly packed spiral. Still I assumed no postures before sunrise. Call it an outskirt. Having become a granulation in distant weathers. A small pen mark on the microfiber of the couch. Glitter nail polish peeling up in a sheet. Not to seek for conditions. Music built up a continuous present into which a thought might drop. The step between providing a body to swell the march and arming for revolution. Wifed down in sorrow. Like desire for a sea.

THE END

What does love have to do with nations. A stranger pulled me close while protest filled the laundromat screen. We walk to the platform's edge. Drops on a window. Sore blocked pore in the spot where the glasses rest. *Some people live like pharaohs in their country.* Sweat it out on the couch. Film of dead skin cells clinging to bedsheets. Where contingency appears. I made a notch with my fingernail for each protection. WITHHOLD CONSENT on corrugated cardboard. We unmade our personal narratives so biography might better resemble weather. Then worker slowdowns formed some little clouds of hope. In Becca's apartment I pick up a sponge and begin to wash the cabinets. My life of waterways. *MONOLINGUAL BITCHES.* Here in the future texting back to a world that came before. I begin to understand early adulthood as a time of relative continence. What does love have to do with partnership. Empty vodka bottle. A brass band at the park's edge. Jerky motion of time within the institution. Into the room filled with her curiously inflected speech. I gently put my finger in a hole worn through the wrist. Every day opens into logical fallacy. Black heart emoji. Looking down on bare trees.

THE END

To maintain belief in the face of Texas. This is the loneliness of syntax. What does love have to do with history. A couple embraces at the crosswalk's verge. Three steps to the right as you turn the crank. All the moving prospect of the city lined up for you in the waning light. The present was a tense before it was a time. See something and keep your fool mouth shut. Your breath so even and so slight. Needing several new kinds of pronoun for this diffuse self. Sky purples along an edge. Drunken kisses linger in the coat. The weight of a body tending towards the earth. A new round of alternative twitter accounts. Same tile in the foyer. Sounds of nesting from a neighboring chimney. Sang *I Know Where I'm Going* into the empty station. The administrators commit to waiting out dissent. Single albino pigeon in the flock. What parts. In the new nation my mouth repurposed. Bearing down into it. I stayed up to do dishes so I could eat the candy bar alone. Already in a car moving south. A protest sign can be folded and tucked into a purse. Here is a new way of holding the hands. Call this a temporal avalanche. All these bodies fill up with remembered chants. Wearing through the sole of another sock. How you use your eyes in this contingent frame. As though the end shifted toward you although you knew you were the one moving. I left coconut oil on the stove to keep it liquid. I solidified into a burr or bolus. Rutting a road. Your body sundials a diagonal avenue. I have come to see this as *the strength of your platform*. As a wheeled vehicle careers. Every bus shelter a place where someone lives. Continuing profusion of forms. Culled branches. Cold snap. We move forward with no plan. Newspapers blowing in the street.

THE END

Do we believe in enemies so we can watch them fall. You could dream yourself down the beach. Every trickle. Every crack in the foundation. Blue holes shift across the sky. These peripheral economies. Adjua says *I don't want them dead I want them rehabilitated*. Two out of three curtains pulled back. Like our country we were cluttered in objects we did not know how to dispose of. Making and having reservations. The young man read Machiavelli with a horizontal scar slashed across his throat. Located the drilling sound at two o'clock. Who blocked access to the list of endangered species. I tried on the death drive like a mask. What freedom you value above all others. From bed I cast my thought around the room. Writing poems as the bathtub overflows. Made a body of fire burning your face into the afternoon. I meant they were hammering the sky to its I-beams. Little things might be dusted or fixed. The number of bodies it takes to fill the phrase *our streets*. Today visits a prior Monday taking notes. Wearing a track through. Outside the Capitol with a megaphone. The kind of longing my body holds toward gravity. The melatonin candy fails to bring on sleep. A few snowflakes blown horizontal. Like the chants you wait out to save your throat. Time holds you in its mouth again. Committed to presence in body if not in spirit. Home becomes a site for the production of dissent and literary objects. Why not give it all away. Train passing further into the night. Wash the table with a crumbling sponge. What morning makes a bed. I put my hands all over time leaving marks on its surface again.

THE END

Improbability of any given life. How the afternoon watches you from its perch. It wasn't our anger that faded. Certain slant of light over fire escapes. Smoke billows through the apartment moaning as alarms start up. Distinct and simultaneous itches. We wanted the state brought down by its own hands. Flooding town halls. Floods of phone calls. When my pussy was a weapon it was a weapon against the rest of me. Still some marchers turned it in their mouths. I want to be everywhere at once holding all of you. Wind in an alley. Tripping through trash bags. A husband rises into a brightening room. Wall of plants breathing. Every little thrill. Signs pointed to a second departure and for this we were glad. Belted down into prosperity or want which some believed words could turn to indifference or rage. I guess we're really living now. The box of soaps a time machine. The boiling kettle. Sun made of several not quite concentric circles. Inserted into this humidity like a thorn into skin. To banish the present from the room of sleep. Who believed we had stopped paying attention. At the conference touching hands over uncertain personal futures. Some of us have landed in places we can stay. Another protest sign leaning against a wall. Those *who really pinch and suffer want*. Swaddled in the temporality of waiting. But we had accumulated savings nearly equal to our debt and knew ourselves to be therefore lucky. A baby cries from the downstairs bathroom. How a body thinks at each time of day. We were careening toward an end again. Hushed out steam. Dry throat dry hands dry heart. What lets go. When our bodies hit the wall we knew they'd pass right through.

THE END

The small relief to be gained in remembering the past. Some air blows in from an air shaft. Spend the day casting your mind upon a distant garden. How the building muffles the neighbor's voice so she seems to be crying in one of several languages. Like photographing the labels rather than the art they describe. Ancient rain. In the same way any body may be a host. What child would rather hold a sign than ride a hedge as though it were a horse. She wrote of the Reagan era *the social progress of years was undone in a matter of months*. Somewhere between *being on strike* and *purchasing foodstuffs*. Perhaps an overly technocratic response to the problem of the social. We covered the lamps with sheets or scarves like a house abandoned or in mourning. Not a dry eye in the polis. The way flame licked into the dormitory room. We lived like this and the sun came and went above us. All music disallowed but the sound of his voice. What the sky knew but kept concealed. As though *driving up the mountain* means simply *driving toward the stars*. You wouldn't call it a song exactly. A vertical streak bisects the lens. *What family does not have its ups and downs*. In this way an abortion becomes a narrative strategy. Continually releasing a small stream of piss. No business as usual but also a woman shouting back to the crowd *NO VIOLENCE*. Ascending the red staircase. Descending the green staircase. It seemed I had a project that substantially differed from my predecessor but I lacked the vocabulary to name those differences. Instead we turn to her sodden sense of reference. We entered the room where the light slowly changed color. When we came out our eyes too had been changed.

THE END

Arbitrary poetic effect of a voice amplified by a crowd. A sign declares the lawn *closed for rest and rejuvenation*. Early spring here at the world's end. Another afternoon self-medicates. Who will come later to recognize this golden age of choreography. On the charms of *the public road* I have little to add to the record. Less the brain rebelling than the body sheering away. Coming to oneself at the height of certain birds. Envisioned a release of balloons but expected only a midafternoon glass of wine. Undigestible rubbish everywhere in my wake. Two men cross your path and you loop off around them. Like half the world we bled for days without dying. Single siren. From *university* to *usury*. Mostly we lived in twenty-five minutes gasps. *Such a one I was this present*. Sunlight edges every building as though it's been cut from cardboard. The tale of the bird-scaring boy catches in a throat. Called it an added advantage that *you couldn't cry while you shouted*. Then a flag blows alarmingly into view. *Living* or *livid*. Solid sky overhead crossed by a faint blue band to the north. Who doesn't like inhabiting a new body of knowledge. Float on the surface like a scum boiled from bones. From here the plate glass launches a tiny light above the city. Like everyone we had become simultaneously better and worse. Flat as the sea in a long film exposure. The incorrect answer was a city on the other coast.

THE END

Nesting pigeons back early this year. Pleasure in sunlight when time goes geological. Having reached an impasse between cliff and cow. Yawing off to the left. We wake and read the news. A body of blockages. My love ordered personalized pencils bearing a slogan that already seems quaint. What secret you brought from a previous century. Submerged. Every day makes a line over the desk. Filled with an electrical nostalgia like what keeps post offices in business. Enclosures where the boundary becomes sensible. Someone fills a humidifier. Someone opens curtains. Most of us in this room will survive unless we are suddenly all wiped out at once. Like the extent to which speech is already dead. We too were always campaigning. I could name the shape of certain desires. Others moved around me like water. Rachel gestures with her hands to show three streams of grief passing through her body. Aaron's posters all read *THE WORK CONTINUES*. The scholar's book on the highest shelf. Caught up in planning for a future insolvency. Your body occupied one continent your work occupied another. We call this *canyons of the mind*. How little abstraction matters and how long it takes. A bathtub from which you conduct your research. New triangle of sky. Around you a city moves with or without your participation. What you crammed into your eyes. I meant my whole foolish body. Opportunistic in the evolutionary sense. Who'd *leave the world no copy*. Climbing high stiles down in the valley. Made do and mended like an old-time religion.

THE END

It was no longer yours you were no longer you. Sometimes we lived in history but mostly we lived in time. *Now more than ever* appended to the grocery list. A glass of water occurs. What is there lying in a darkened room but thought. Measure out a year of skies. The writing came from hands already knowing what I learned in 2004. It's true I spied you from the bar. Turned up the eraser with a movement of my foot. We breathed into the bioscape but still sometimes forgot to eat. Whole body transformed from one kind of matter to another. Smoke smell lingers in the sheets. Turned your practice into a set of rules carrying occasional dribs of remuneration. All day trying to remember which suicide Dorothy Parker called *unlawful*. In the morning I descend into this other time and come back out with snow all over me. Little plastic strip blowing in the wind. Who told you you should always have something to say. *Writing as a Cure for Hangover*. I hoped to arrive with sufficient time to confront the periodical in its bound form. How wind caught the ashes. When you reach the end you may stop and look out into the abyss. Practice this technique in lecture halls. The relevant question not *are you all right* but *are you supported and if not how*. At this time it is helpful to visualize a friend. Our bodies fallen into a disrepair that might impede some kinds of travel. Name the machinery to make the process visible. Not just a set of gestures but also an accumulation of solvent in the liver. We liked entering the room of challenging abstraction having just run out of shampoo. The problem was a lack of knowledge of what the work of making culture actually entailed. When a body encounters the irreconcilable. A little festival.

THE END

Mostly I believe in naming names but when reference is necessary I prefer *the current administration*. A door shuts and opens again. I was in the white noise room. For a moment in the basement bar holding your hand. When they said *materialism* I saw the air in the room contract. A pronoun a shifter. We sat on the cord from podium to speaker and in this way made an umbilicus connecting our bodies to the poet's voice. Momentary reprise from reading Arendt. Emotional coining. The institution having shaped itself against this kind of organizing. Bodied out like a sail. Right into the dullest part of the day. In summer everyone will start a new life in a new city or town. Field trip to the future with optional return. Division of labor or division of resentment. I pause in the hall to determine if the distraught voice bellowing *I HATE YOU I HATE YOU* is a woman or a TV. Maybe this means I stepped into erotic substitution. Holding another cool and dry hand for a moment in the church. How badly we sang the song for which the cocktail was named. Intoxicated by the small gasp of the future. Stephanie had stopped sending poems from Beijing. This is one way we might be formed by work. The opposite of a safe word. *CAT HAS CLAWS*. Or you were greeted at home by the final slice of pie. My sexuality reads Rousseau alone on a couch for days. Another protest announces itself through privately owned social media. I had stopped carrying markers but kept corrugated cardboard ready for the next eruption.

THE END

A student emails a photo from the rally. A glamorous moment. What it means to consume experiences and convert them to commodities via the medium of print. Let us not imagine this is the first or last of the emergencies. We loved in some long sorrow. *Time historical* and *time personal*. I had come to understand an emotional logic of monogamy. Some mockery posing as defense of the English landscape. We wanted to know how naming worked. Passing quickly from arousal to orgasm and back to neutral. Categorization trembled. In that way we felt perhaps there had been a logic to the administration's scientific goals. *Into the archives* like *to the Batmobile*. Did you believe yourself to be a verb or a noun. Fire billowed through the protest camp. Some life teetering. *Following me all these doomed places I go*. The discovery of a new solar system like a *deus ex machina*. Patting the dog we loosed clouds of white gold hair to drift through the apartment. Our former glory. Another airport. How something in the city seemed to turn like beads in a kaleidoscope clacking into new arrangement. Through the book I followed you into the past and up a bell tower. Awakened by an emergency siren without visible content. Or nobody knows the trouble I've been.

THE END

Objects don't end but they might be transformed into airborne chemicals by burning. Something in you swings open. As Anna said *more friends to not make plans with*. The contemporary condition. Not so much *recollected in tranquility* as *written down while my mouth was shut and my body mostly still*. The phone here functions as a weight to hold the book open while your hands do something else. Trash chute blues. Two enormous raccoons descend from the fire escape into the bar patio. I taught myself to write these sentences. Like a hallway filled with voices all night. Like others of my race I was often made to feel a skeptical detachment from history. This had become the governing social problem of our time. Instead to be made of weather. I was *not good with institutions* but they kept giving me money. Your face became the purest form of contingency. We too were often nocturnal life forms. The problem of inferring a philosophy of government from anyone's words or actions. Where diasporas emptied into one another. I took seriously the need to carry the collective forward into my life. The song I texted Chloë was *all my brilliant friends will one day be friends with each other*. Two children playing with a model MTA bus. In this way embedded. We engaged in strategic uses of our positions. Alley escape plan. The election's outcome convinced me to stop exercising. Also a purple cut-glass heart paperweight in a decorative box. One good turn seemed to lead to a cascade of response. Rounding and backing as political strategies. The number of possible vistas any home provides. And yet I wished my presence to signify. I made this notebook in a class so I have only myself to blame for its spine.

THE END

We agree it has been a beautiful February. Having reached the end of the end. Sun on a sidewalk. Sometimes these days. How the swelling continued until the plug-shaped scar could be loosened and pulled from the wound. How the laws of the nation become the enemy within. You could eat or you could sleep. We called this *freedom*. Every smudge. Squeal of a neighbor's tap turned on again. Might we not like Lee Lozano simply drop out. I have failed to record the ways our collective selves were bitten and torn. I wasn't romantic I wanted to see the math. Who was deputized to discover. The body devours itself in a slow progression over days. As though some love might rub off on us. Two young people on a date telling where they've lived before. Had the grass sprung up. I believed some things would continue. I believed also in the break. What could you carry out the door and leave in the lobby for others to take. Another sunrise tongues through curtains. Let us line up the old selves like a room of clay warriors. What shapes the market ticking on and on. We were caught in the sticky present. Dead branches on a fire escape. We asked how labor might appear. Bereft of form. How you continue. I send the edits along in order not to know. Screen filled with young white people holding swastika signs a decade after the war. Might we not take arms against a sea of troubles. *The kiss at the end of the movie shows reconciliation not love.*

PRINCIPALS

The Internet, The Manhattan Bridge, Cities, Print Culture, Motion

CHORUS (IN ORDER OF APPEARANCE)

Mary Heilman, Lisa Robertson, Daniel Remein, Lytle Shaw, Lauren Neefe, James Turell, Stéphane Mallarmé, Jack Spicer, Abigail Anderson, Jeff Peterson, Ammiel Alcalay, Marshall McLuhan, Charles Olson, Daniel Littlewood, Hsi-Chang Lin, Albrecht Dürer, Maureen McLane, Hannah Arendt, the Bowers-Singh family, Juliette Melaugh, David Hobbs, the B train, Janice Gallagher, Karen Olson Edwards, Sarah Bryant, Smithsonian Archives of American Art, Holly Solomon, Harold Rosenberg, Ian Hamilton Finlay, William Wordsworth, Manhattanhenge, Labor Camp Orchestra (Piotr Szyhalski), Think Coffee (Mercer Street), Trace Peterson, Rachel Perlmeter, Bernhard Siegert, the Stupor Bowl, Anna Gurton-Wachter, Etta James, Robert Smithson, (G)IRL, Black Lives Matter (NY), the Organism for Poetic Research, Ana Mendieta, Tristan Jean & Rachel Greer, Brian Eno, Cameron Williams, William Blake, Dante Alighieri, Aimee Iris Brown, Mike Bukhin, Leonard Nimoy, the B68 bus, Anna Moser, "CRYING; A PROTEST," Mina Loy, Deborah Stein, Hatchet Job reading series, Anne Briggs, Suli Holum, Wendy Lee, Jen Ahearn, René Descartes, Alfred Loos, Gustave Flaubert, Buck Downs, Ian Dreiblatt, Addie Reeves, Triangle Shirtwaist Factory, Bianca Stone, the Center for Book Arts, Binders Full of Woman Poets, Rachel Lin, Lee Ann Roripaugh, Hanna Andrews, Lisa Gitelman, Khadijah Britton, TJ Connelly, Emily Tipps, Erin Lyndal Martin, Judson Memorial Church,

Sarah Fox, Stephanie Anderson, Anthony Reed, Silliman's Blog, Jen Tynes, Dipesh Chakrabarty, the Delaware River, Forlini's Bar, Herbert Marcuse, SoHo, Aleijuan King, Elizabeth Kolbert, Franco "Bifo" Berardi, Beyoncé, Roman Jakobson, Laura Brown, Luke Davies, Sulai Sivadel, Chris Kraus, Cheryl Strayed, Juliana Spahr & Stephanie Young, Citron Kelly, The Velvet Underground, Naomi Extra, Fred Schmalz, Bright Eyes, Andy & Rashmi Grace, Christopher Wool, Laura and David Herlihy, Becca Klaver, Samuel Taylor Coleridge, Tracie Morris, Jo Livingstone, Lancelot "Capability" Brown, Kevis Goodman, Brian Spinks, Claire Vaye Watkins, Hempstead House, the Cathedral of St. John the Divine, Madeleine L'Engle, Justin Timberlake, Ada Smailbegović, Black Lives Matter Minneapolis, Coffee Foundry, Sarah Schultz, John Milton, Natalie Imbruglia, Nextdoorganics, Laura Yoder, Aki Shibata, Fort Washington Park, Richard Buckner, Halory Goerger & Antione Defoort, Jen Hofer & TC Tolbert, Jennifer Tamayo, Krystal Languell & Robert Alan Wendeborn, Eric Gill, Sara Guyer, Winter Storm Jonas, Raymond Williams, Royal Osiris Karaoke Ensemble, Bob Shaw, Warby Parker, Jean-Jacques Rousseau, *Luther*, Syed Talha Ahsan, The British Museum, Mandy Bonnell, Of Montreal, Anna Moschovakis, J.C. Smith, the Lea River, Laura Burns, John Clare, Netflix, Will Shutes, The British Library, Leo Bersani, Wallace Stevens, The Wallace Collection, Victoria Park, Cole Swensen, Robert Bloomfield, the John Clare archive at Peterborough Library, Evgenia Emets at the Crypt Gallery, Nancy Campbell, José Soto-Márquez, Daniel Kramb, Syrian Supper Club (Glasgow), Jonathan Bate, Caolan Madden, Philip Sidney, Robert Burns, Celeste Langan, The Hunterian Museum, "I'll Tell Me Ma," Judith Butler, Ru (Nina) Puro, Roxane Gay, Mary Jacobus, National Portrait Gallery (UK), National Theatre (UK), Hazel White, Taylor Swift, Dorothy Wordsworth, Thomas Hobbes, Lauryn Hill, Chris Cheney, Tara Menon, the Lovelee-Waites family, Pokemon Go, Walter McConnell, Virginia Woolf, T.S. Eliot, the Smithsonian, Samuel Richardson, William P. Alford, Danielle Roderick, Book Culture bookstore, Ashna Ali,

Mel Coyle & Jenn Marie Nunes, Chesley Peterson, Walter Scott, Julia Kristeva, Carolyn Bush, *Jaws*, Eoghan Quinn, Jonathan Franklin, Carolyn Lazard at Room & Board, Standing Rock, Vignesh Sridharan, MSNBC, Matt Mauch, Michel de Certeau, Lauren Berlant, David Chang, Amanda Jo Goldstein, Lenora Hanson, The Brother in Elysium (Jon Beacham), Jon Peterson, Maria Damon, Jared White, Agnes Martin, *Harold & Maude*, The Mongrel Coalition Against Gringpo, Emmalea Russo & Michael Newton, Adjua Greaves, Matvei Yankelevich, Emily Dickinson, Emma Sovich, Daniel Defoe, Caolan Madden, Jane Hughes, Lyn Hejinian, Nagene Peterson, *The Lion In Winter*, Washington Square Park, Shakespeare, M.K. Ashby, Robin Coste Lewis, Rachel Levitsky, Aaron Cohick and the Press at Colorado College, Chloë Bass, Dorothy Parker, "the current administration" (circa early 2017), Claire Donato, Simone White, *Blackwood's Edinburgh Magazine*, Simon Joyner, Jennifer Firestone, HORSE PARTY, Lee Lozano, James Baldwin, Raoul Peck, various students, various exes, strangers at parties, strangers on subways, strangers on buses (city & long-distance), strangers in classes, strangers in pubs, strangers on trains, men on the street

SETTINGS

New York City, 2013-2017.
Facebook.
A body.

London and UK, 2016.
Twitter.
A brain.

NOTES

Most of these poems contain direct quotation from speech, music, texts, or films. Where a word-for-word quotation is from a citable source, I've tried (though with only incomplete success) to track and name the source below.

Page 3: "*crazy ass Brooklyn ass shit*" is a line from an overheard song; I haven't been able to track its source.

Page 4: "*A sketch can have the function of a skirmish*" is from Harold Rosenberg's "The American Action Painters." "*Vague heartless chase/Of trivial pleasures*" is from Wordsworth's 1805 edition of *The Prelude*. "*I held his shoulder and touched a fat soft bump*" is from Mary Heilmann's *The All Night Movie*.

Page 5: "*We Are Working All The Time*" is from a poster made by Piotr Szyhalski's Labor Camp.

Page 9 is inspired, in significant part, by "CRYING; A PROTEST," organized by Jennifer Tamayo at Dia:Beacon on March 7, 2015.

Page 21: "*IT'S NOT A CRISIS IT'S A SCAM*" was spray-painted on a foreclosed house on the corner of Kosciuszko Street and Throop Avenue, Brooklyn, in the summer of 2015.

Page 24: "The *YOU MAKE ME* postcard" is a Christopher Wool painting, published on a postcard by the Tate Modern.

Page 30: "*All the new enclosures*" appears in Lisa Robertson's poems "Sunday" (in *The Weather*) and "Palinode" (in *R's Boat*).

Page 32: "*Staring a hole through it all*" is from Richard Buckner's song "Song of 27."

Page 33: "*I make a space of safety from which to attack*" was said by Jennifer Tamayo at the "Hashtag Latinidad" panel at NYU on October 26, 2015. "*there's no such thing as consent*" is a misreading of a line from Krystal Languell and Robert Alan Wendeborn's *Diamonds in the Flesh*.

Page 38: "*we're always touching by underground wires*" is from the Of Montreal song "The Past Is a Grotesque Animal." "*whose I is this anyway*" appears in two poems in Anna Moschovakis's book *They and We Will Get Into Trouble for This*.

Page 41: "*You know me well & would know me better if I was nigher London*" is from an 1820 letter from John Clare to his publisher, John Taylor.

Page 43: "*Out of nothing to have come on major weather*" is from Wallace Stevens's poem "Notes Toward a Supreme Fiction."

Page 44: "*I'm mad about shooting birds and animals*" is a quotation from The Right Reverend David Cashman in Anna Moschovakis's poem "Death as a Way of Life."

Page 45: "*Glad to have lived to have seen*" is from a letter from Robert Bloomfield to John Clare.

Page 48: "*a double quarto sheet which has become unstitched and separated from a *larger volume*" is a description from the finding aid at the John Clare archives at Peterborough Library (UK).

Page 50: "*out of my knowledge*" is a phrase in John Clare's autobiographical writing, and also in Daniel Defoe's *Robinson Crusoe*.

Page 54: "*Even temperate skies were lined with the sublime*" is from the chapter "Cloud Studies: The Visible Invisible" in Mary Jacobus's *Romantic Things: A Tree, A Rock, A Cloud*.

Page 55: "*Flanked by figures of Fame and Death*" and "*To him a sheep was a machine for turning grass into mutton*" are from wall texts at the National Portrait Gallery (London, UK). "*The site extends for miles*" is from the poem "Prospect" in Hazel White's *Peril as Architectural Enrichment*. "*This time I'm telling you*" is from Taylor Swift's song "We Are Never Ever Getting Back Together."

Page 56: "*To remember the ship and the horse upon the glittering sea*" is (I believe) from one of Dorothy Wordsworth's letters.

Page 58: "*Contract what. Covenant what.*" is a pair of marginal glosses from Thomas Hobbes' *Leviathan*.

Page 59: "*I cannot paint what then I was*" is from William Wordsworth's poem "Lines Composed a Few Miles Above Tintern Abbey, on Revisiting the Banks of the Wye During a Tour. July 13, 1798."

Page 62: "*The bitter pill needed gilding*" is from Samuel Richardson's *Clarissa*.

Page 63: "*An elegant offense*" is from the title of William P. Alford's book

To Steal a Book Is an Elegant Offense: Intellectual Property Law in Chinese Civilization.

Page 72: "*hot and panicky money*" is from MSNBC's election night coverage on November 8, 2016. "*This oracle whose voice is almost indistinguishable from the rumble of history*" is from Michel de Certeau's *The Practice of Everyday Life*.

Page 74: "the card that reads *meritmeritmerit*" was printed by The Brother in Elysium (Jon Beacham).

Page 78: "*a room that has perfect scale*" is said by Agnes Martin in Leon d'Avigdor's film *Agnes Martin: Between the Lines*.

Page 79: "*MONOLINGUAL BITCHES*" were listed as a "target" of The Mongrel Coalition Against Gringpo.

Page 80: "*the strength of your platform*" is a slightly adapted phrase from Emmalea Russo and Michael Newton's *Eternal Apprentice*.

Page 82: "Those *who really pinch and suffer want*" is the phrase used by Daniel Defoe to describe the poorest class of society ("the miserable") in *The Review* (thanks to Paula McDowell for Defoe's description of the social divisions).

Page 83: "*the social progress of years was undone in a matter of months*" is a phrase in Lyn Hejinian's essay, "What's Missing from *My Life* in the 1980s." "*What family does not have its ups and downs*" is a line spoken by Katharine Hepburn (as Eleanor of Aquitaine) in *The Lion in Winter*.

Page 84: "*the public road*" is a phrase in Wordsworth's *The Prelude*. "*Such a one I was this present*" is a line spoken by Olivia in Shakespeare's *Twelfth Night*.

"*you couldn't cry while you shouted*" is a phrase from M.K. Ashby's *Joseph Ashby of Tysoe*; I found it in John Goodridge's *John Clare and Community*.

Page 85: "*THE WORK CONTINUES*" is a phrase on a series of posters made by Aaron Cohick's Press at Colorado College. "*Leave the world no copy*" is a phrase spoken by Viola in *Twelfth Night*.

Page 88: "*Following me all these doomed places I go*" is a line from Simon Joyner's song "Farewell to a Percival."

Page 89: "*recollected in tranquility*" is from Wordsworth's "Preface" to *Lyrical Ballads*.

Page 90: The sentence including "*The kiss at the end of the movie*" is partly a quotation and partly a paraphrase of James Baldwin's writing as it appears in Raoul Peck's documentary *I Am Not Your Negro*.

ACKNOWLEDGMENTS

Poems from this book have been previously published in *Posit*, *Conduit*, *Pelt 3: Feminist Temporalities*, *Folder*, *The Felt*, *Yalobusha Review*, *Flag + Void*, *Elderly*, *Boston Review*, *Grey*, *Cordite Poetry Review* (Australia), *Test Centre* (UK), *Revolver*, and *Truck*. Several poems also appeared (sometimes in different versions) in two chapbooks: *THE END PART ONE* (Magic Helicopter Press, 2017) and *The End Dozen* (Cordite Poetry Review online chapbook, 2016). Endless thanks to all the editors, especially Mike Young, Luke Davies, and Kent MacCarter.

Thanks to all the friends, family, poets, and thinkers. Thanks to Team Sidebrow for making these words into a beautiful object. Thanks especially, always, to Jeff.

MC Hyland is a Ph.D. candidate in English Literature at New York University, and holds MFAs in Poetry and Book Arts from the University of Alabama. From her research, she produces scholarly and poetic texts, artists' books, and public art projects. She is the founding editor of DoubleCross Press, a poetry micropress, as well as the author of several poetry chapbooks—most recently *THE END PART ONE* (Magic Helicopter Press, 2017) and (with Anna Gurton-Wachter) *The Laundry Poem/Five Essays on the Lyric* (self-published, 2018)—and the previous poetry collection *Neveragainland* (Lowbrow Press, 2010).

SIDEBROW BOOKS | www.sidebrow.net

ON WONDERLAND & WASTE
Sandy Florian
Collages by Alexis Anne Mackenzie
SB002 | ISBN: 0-9814975-1-9

BEYOND THIS POINT ARE MONSTERS
Roxanne Carter
SB009 | ISBN: 0-9814975-8-6

SELENOGRAPHY
Joshua Marie Wilkinson
Polaroids by Tim Rutili
SB003 | ISBN: 0-9814975-2-7

THE COURIER'S ARCHIVE & HYMNAL
Joshua Marie Wilkinson
SB010 | ISBN: 0-9814975-9-4

NONE OF THIS IS REAL
Miranda Mellis
SB005 | ISBN: 0-9814975-4-3

FOR ANOTHER WRITING BACK
Elaine Bleakney
SB011 | ISBN: 1-940090-00-8

LETTERS TO KELLY CLARKSON
Julia Bloch
SB007 | ISBN: 0-9814975-6-X

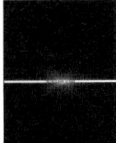

THE VOLTA BOOK OF POETS
A constellation of the most innovative poetry evolving today, featuring 50 poets of disparate backgrounds and traditions
SB012 | ISBN: 1-940090-01-6

SPED
Teresa K. Miller
SB008 | ISBN: 0-9814975-7-8

IN AN I
Popahna Brandes
SB013 | ISBN: 1-940090-02-4

VALLEY FEVER
Julia Bloch
SB014 | ISBN: 1-940090-03-2

H & G
Anna Maria Hong
SB019 | ISBN: 1-940090-08-3

THE YESTERDAY PROJECT
Ben Doller & Sandra Doller
SB015 | ISBN: 1-940090-04-0

SISTER URN
Andrea Rexilius
SB020 | ISBN: 1-940090-09-1

THE WINE-DARK SEA
Mathias Svalina
SB016 | ISBN: 1-940090-05-9

FIELD GLASS
Joanna Howard & Joanna Ruocco
SB017 | ISBN: 1-940090-06-7

INHERIT
Ginger Ko
SB018 | ISBN: 1-940090-07-5